I0468854

Forgiveness
is the way of cleansing the soul
. . . .

Marita Gale

ISBN-10: 1517160790
ISBN-13: 978-1517160791

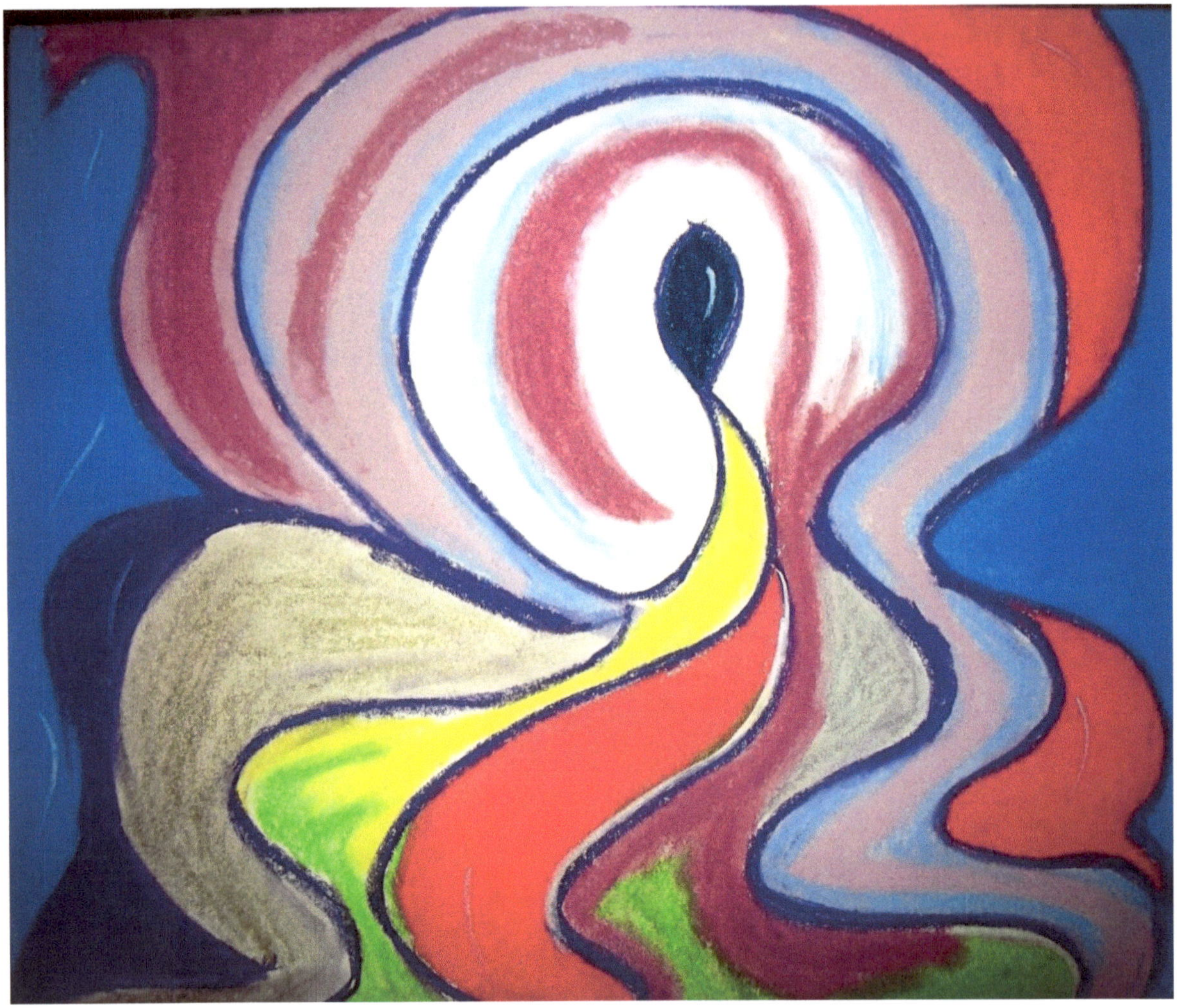

Forgiveness is the way

Of cleansing the soul

So it moves the way

It was meant to move --

With pure joy

The journey begins . . .

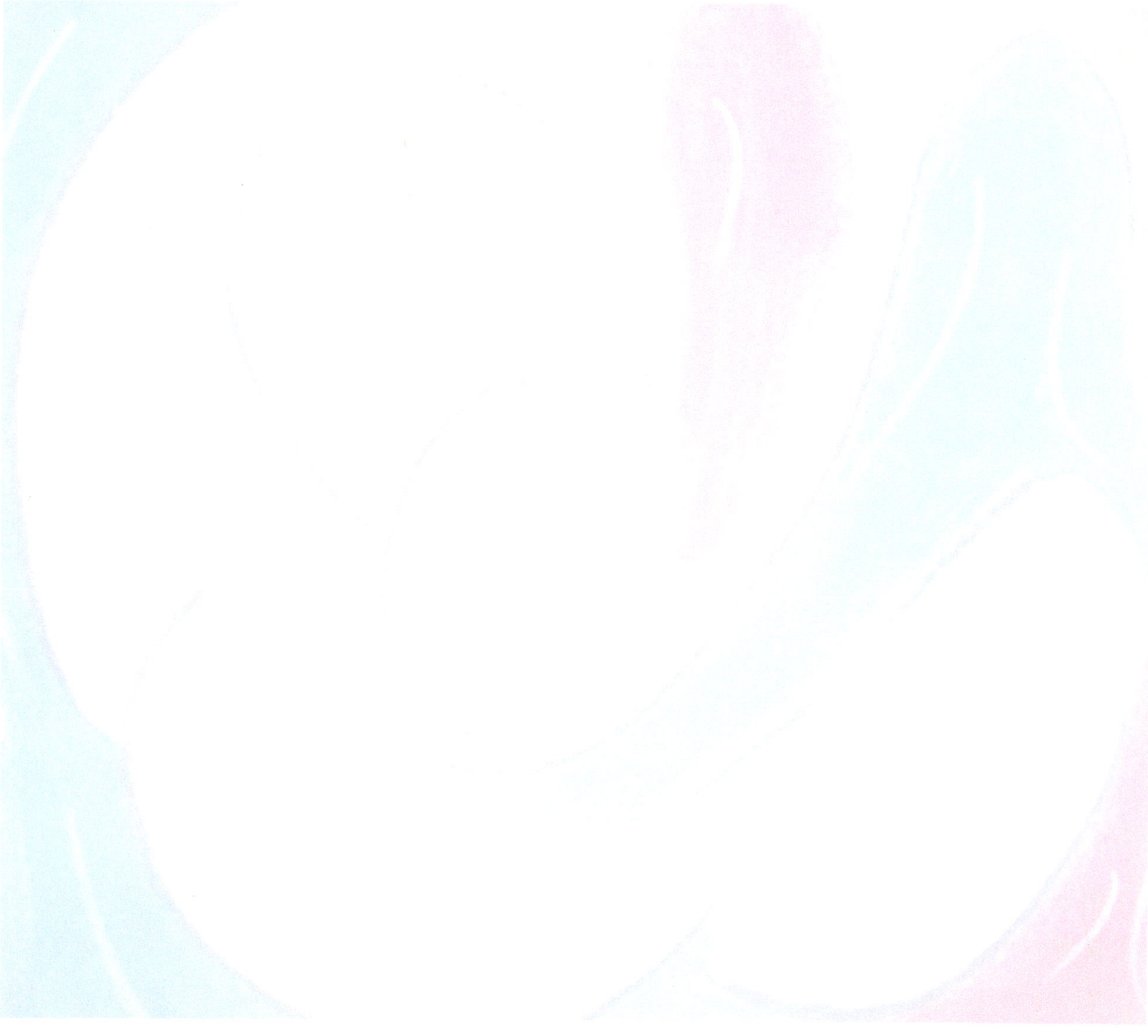

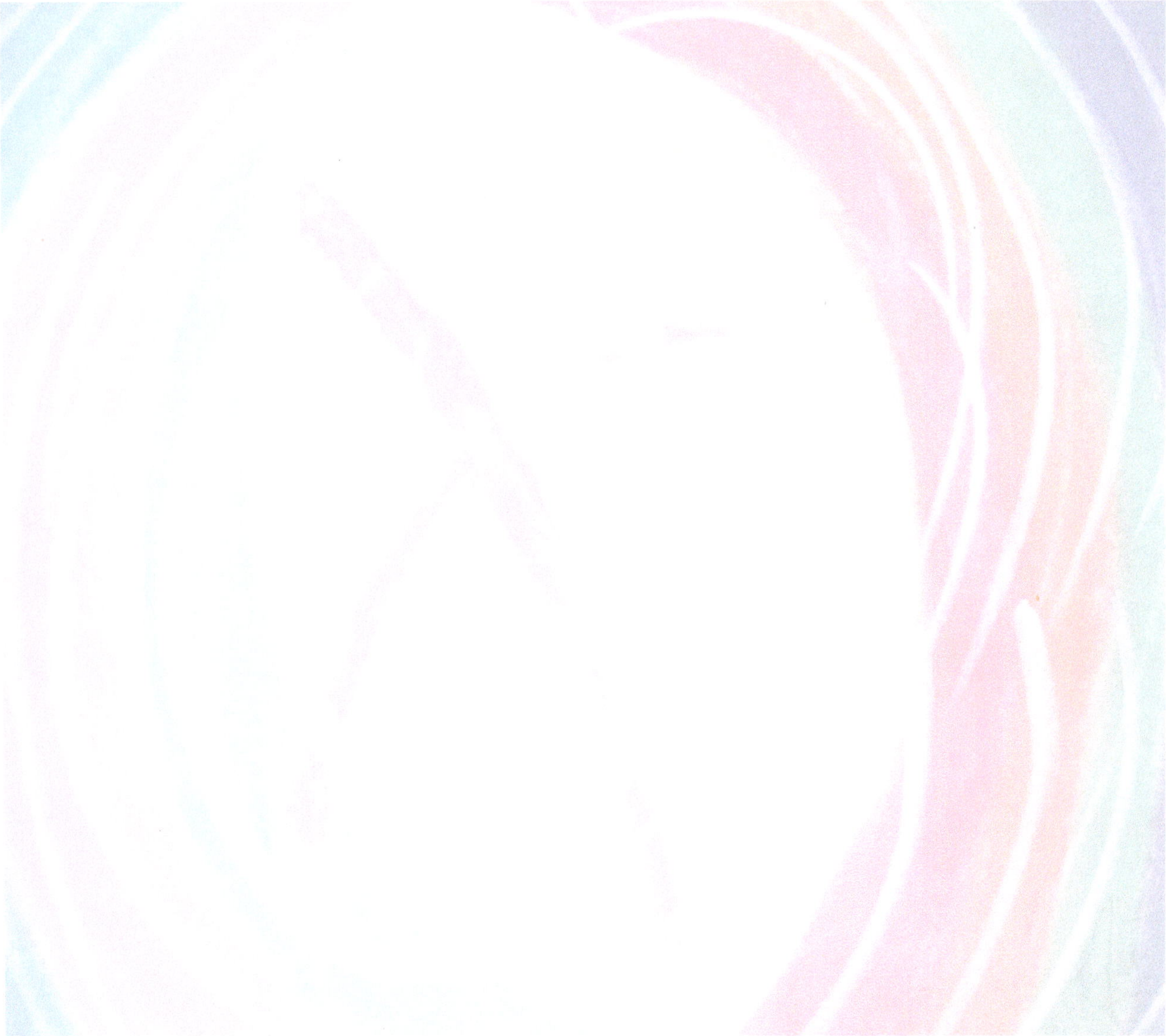

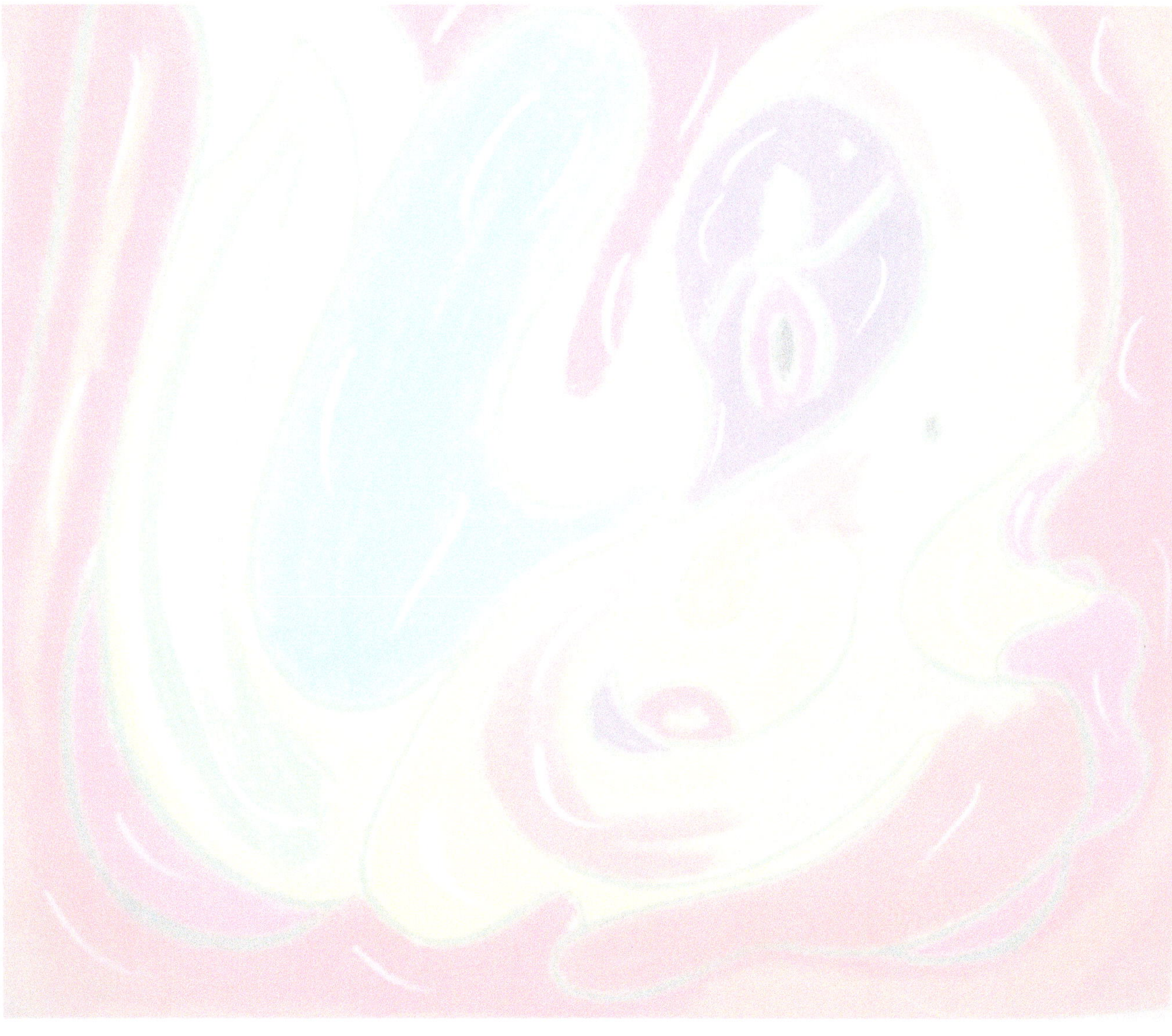

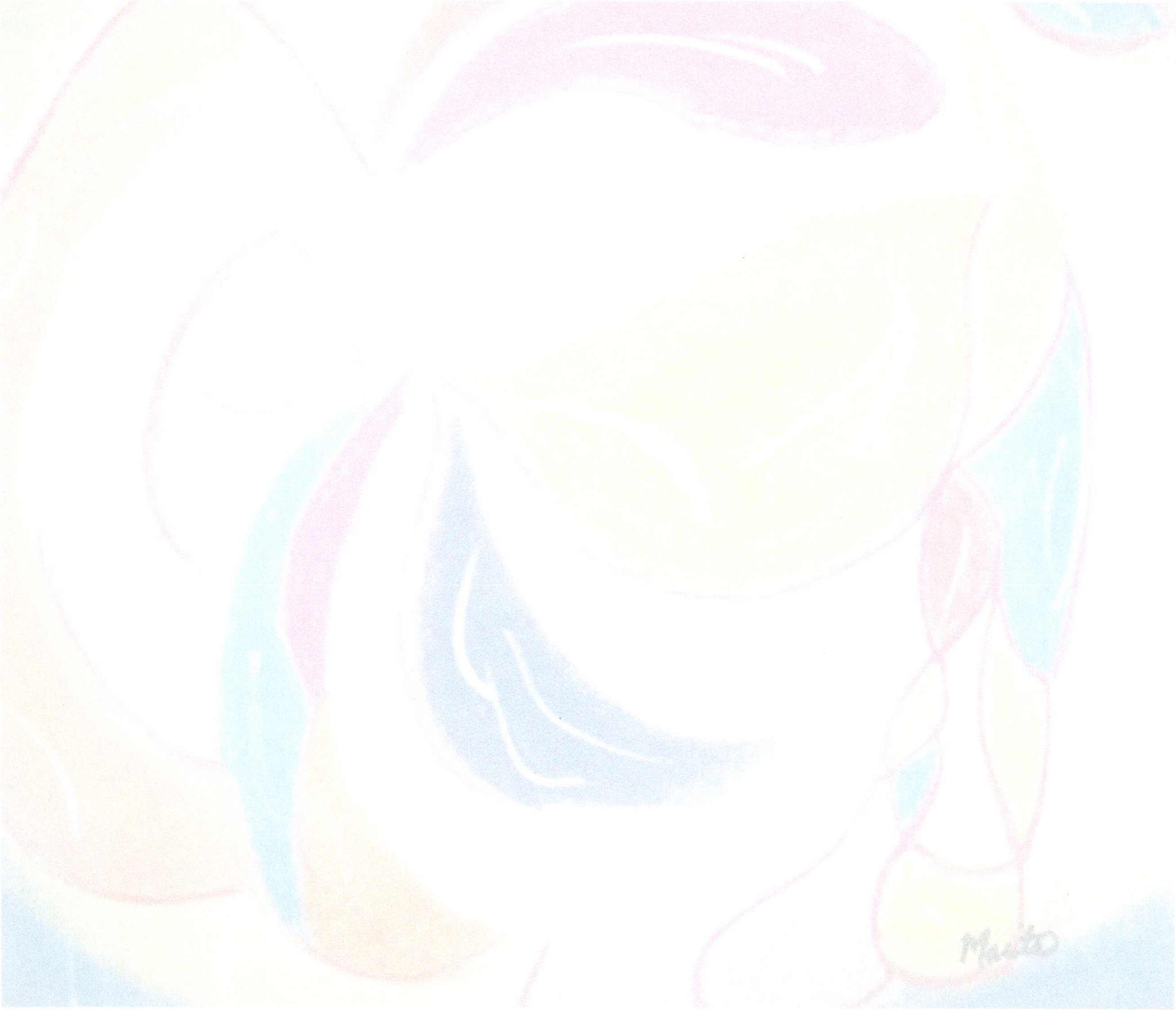

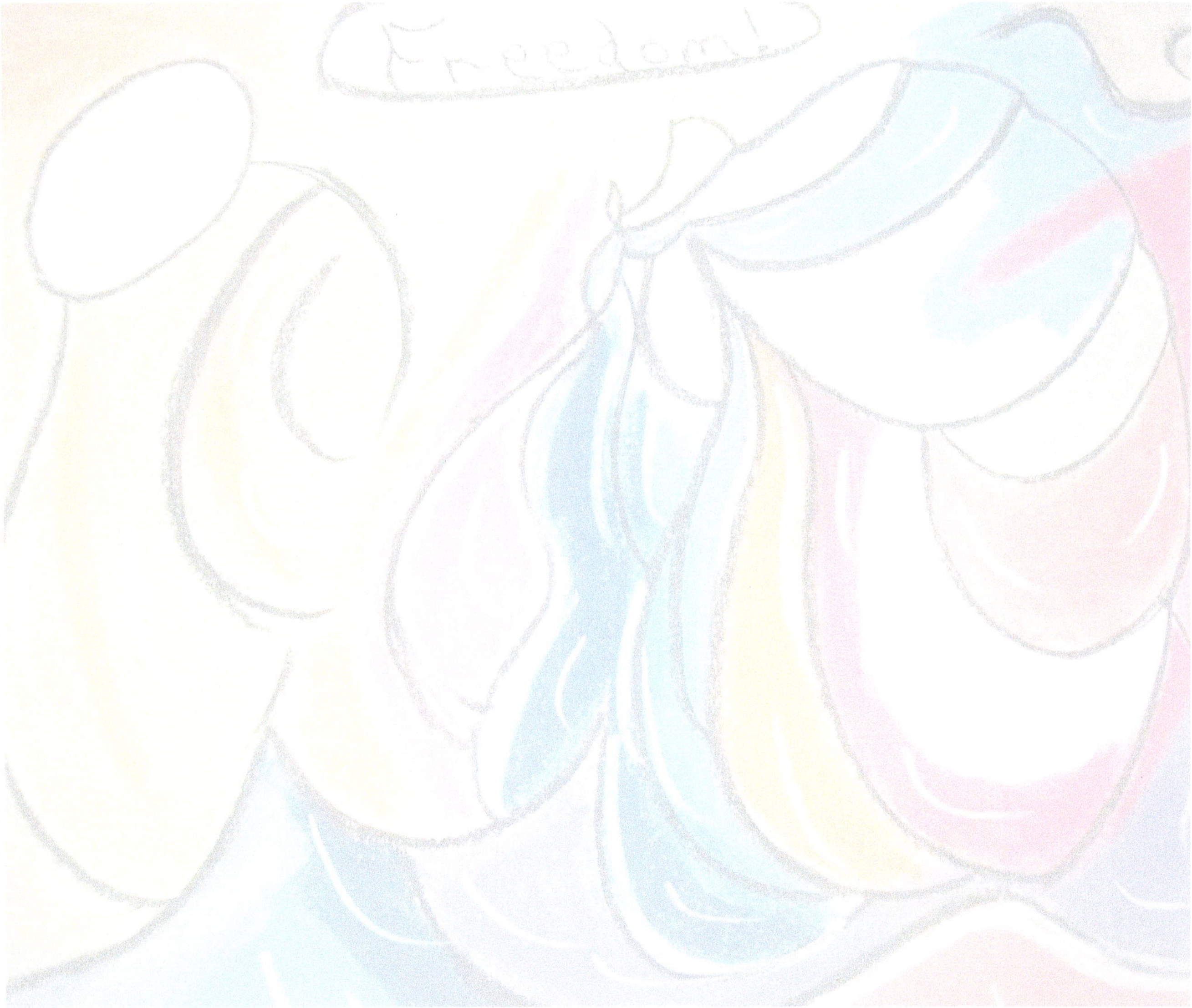

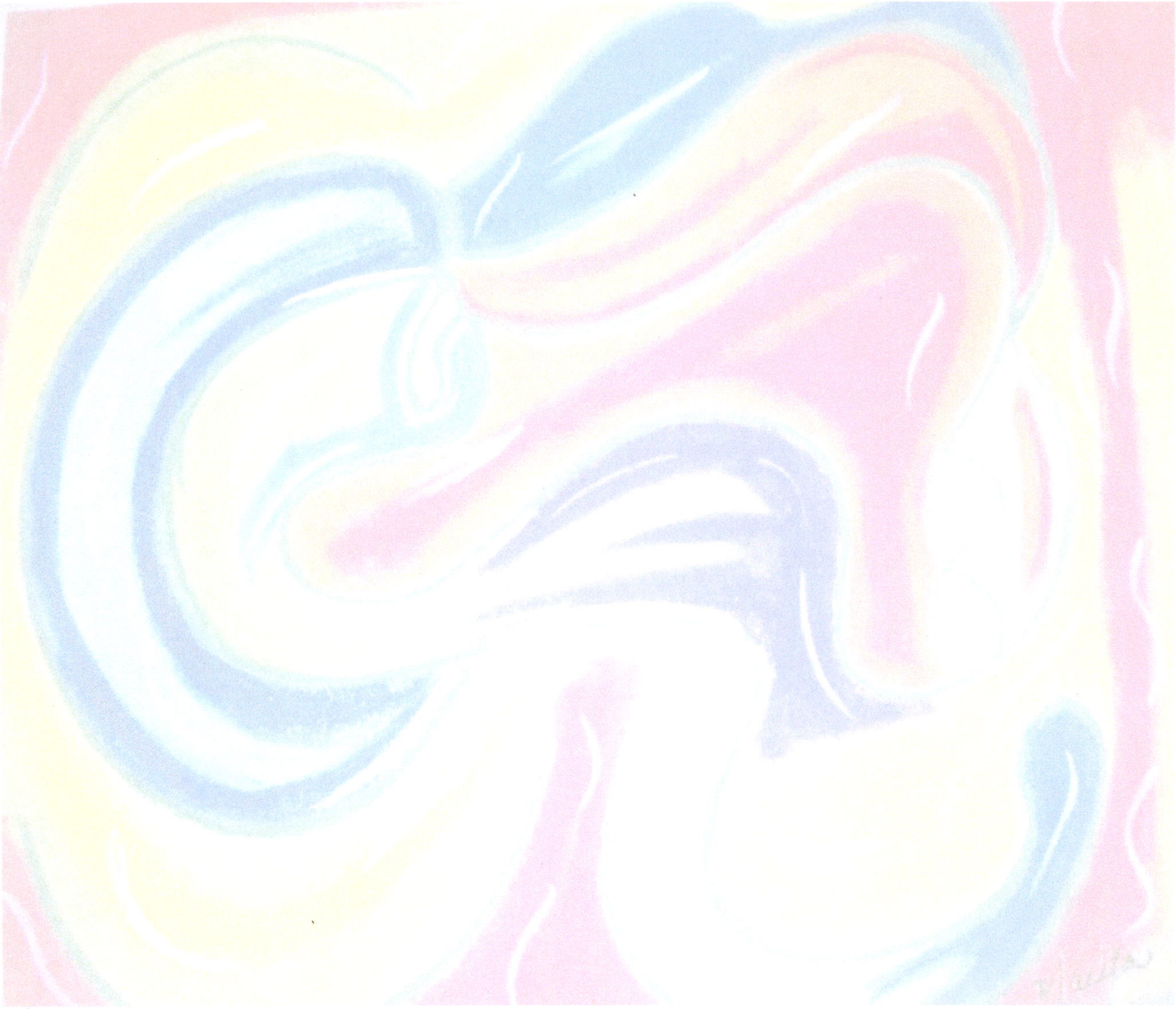

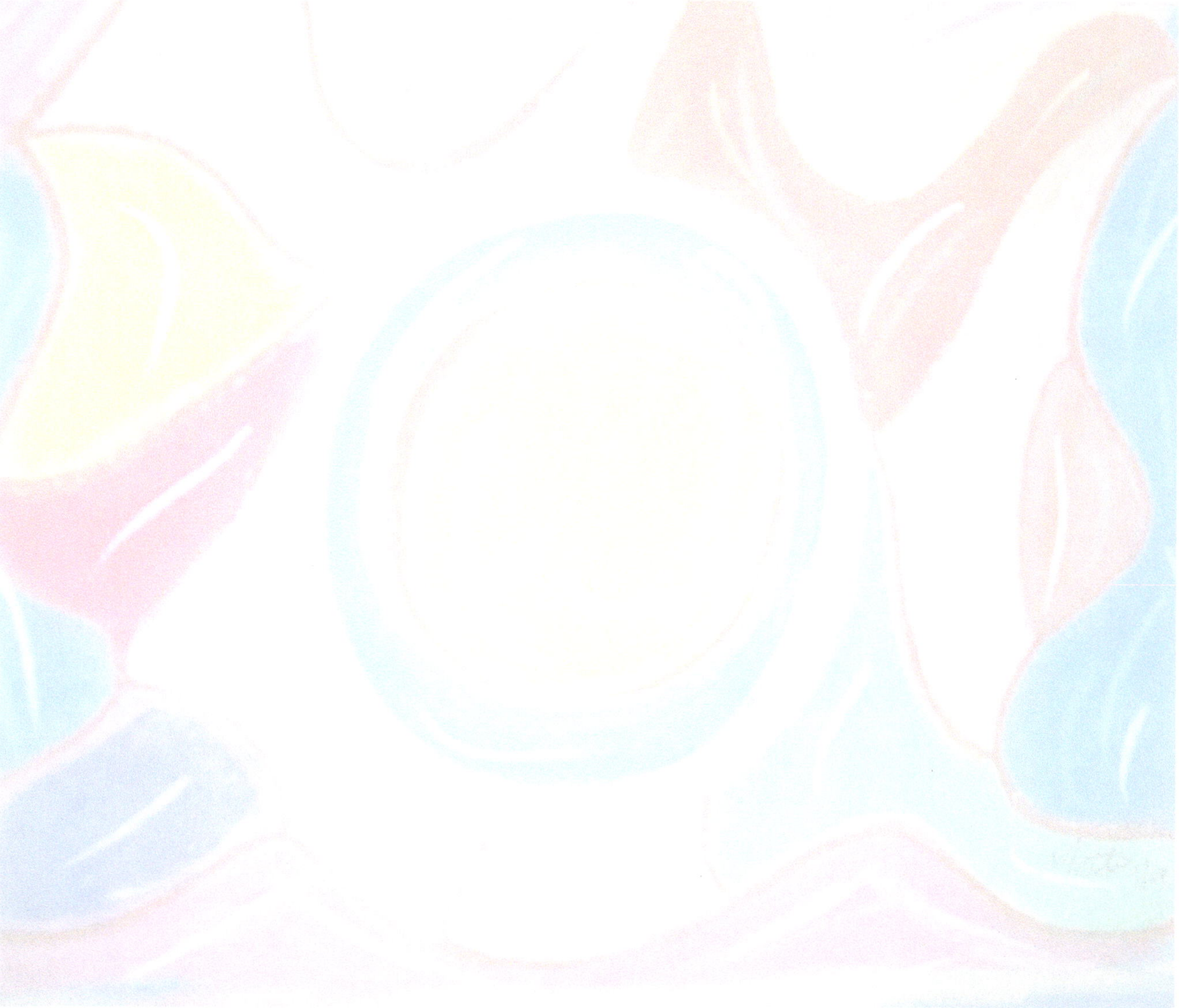

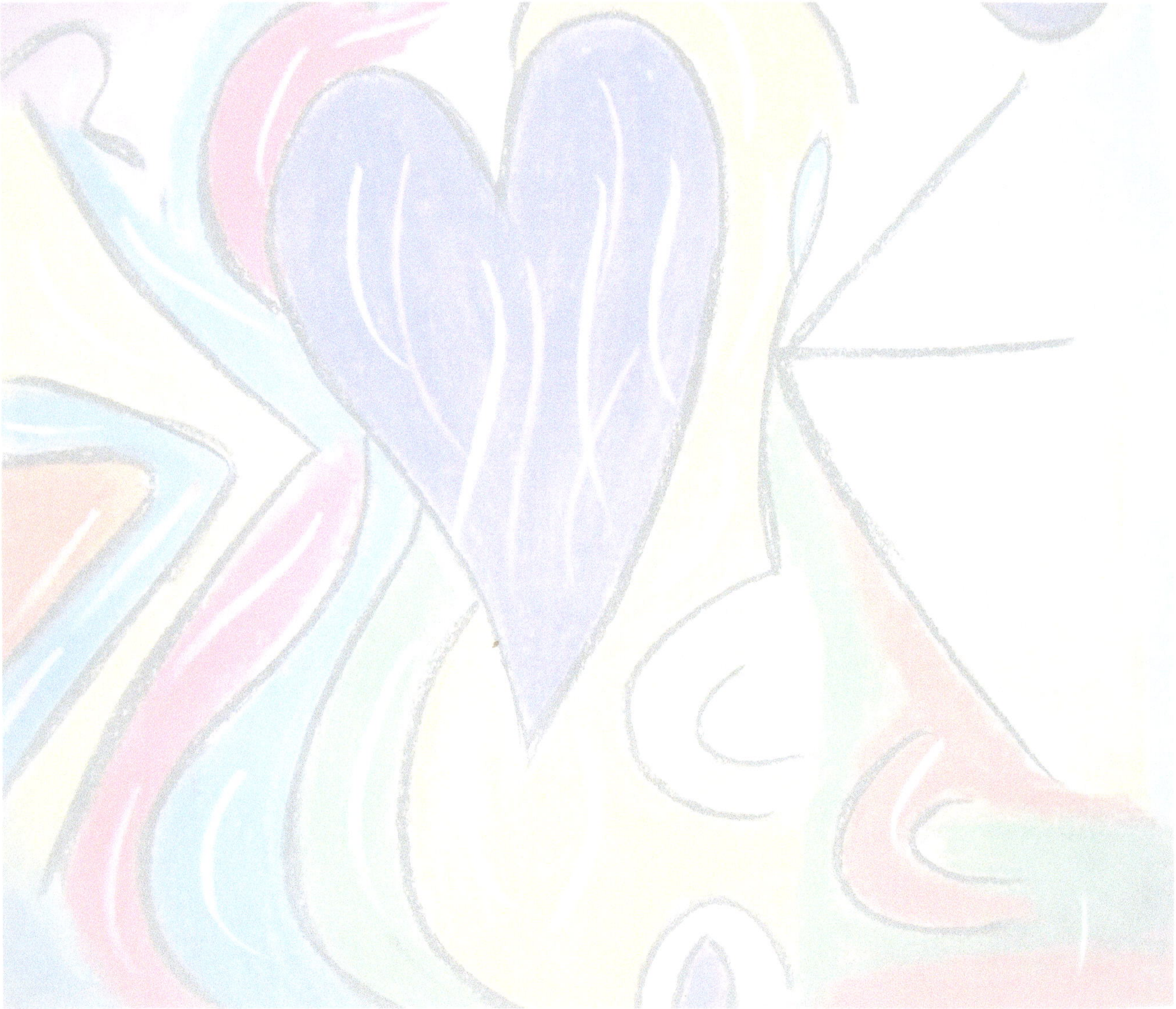

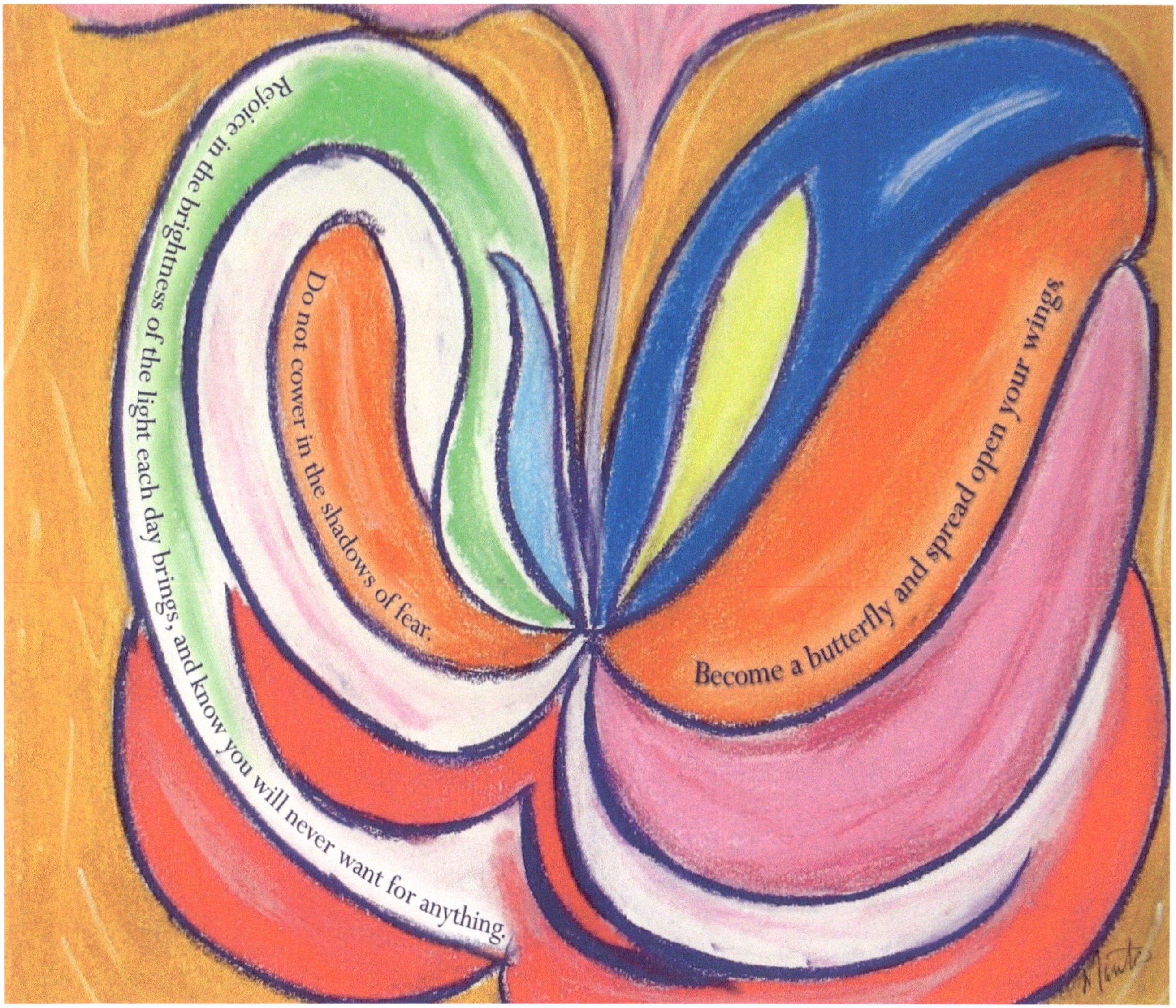

Rejoice in the brightness of the light each day brings, and know you will never want for anything.

Do not cower in the shadows of fear.

Become a butterfly and spread open your wings.

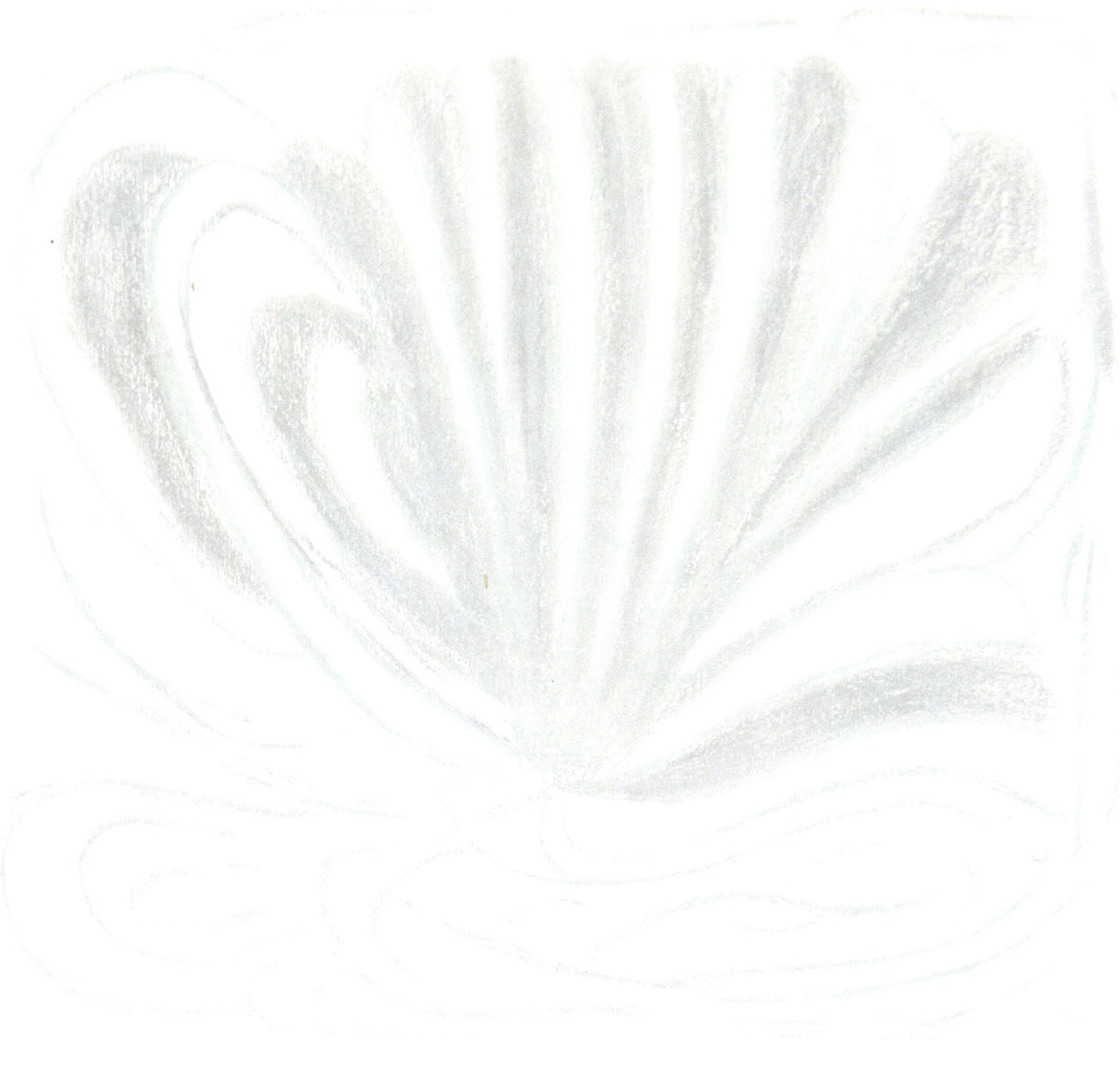

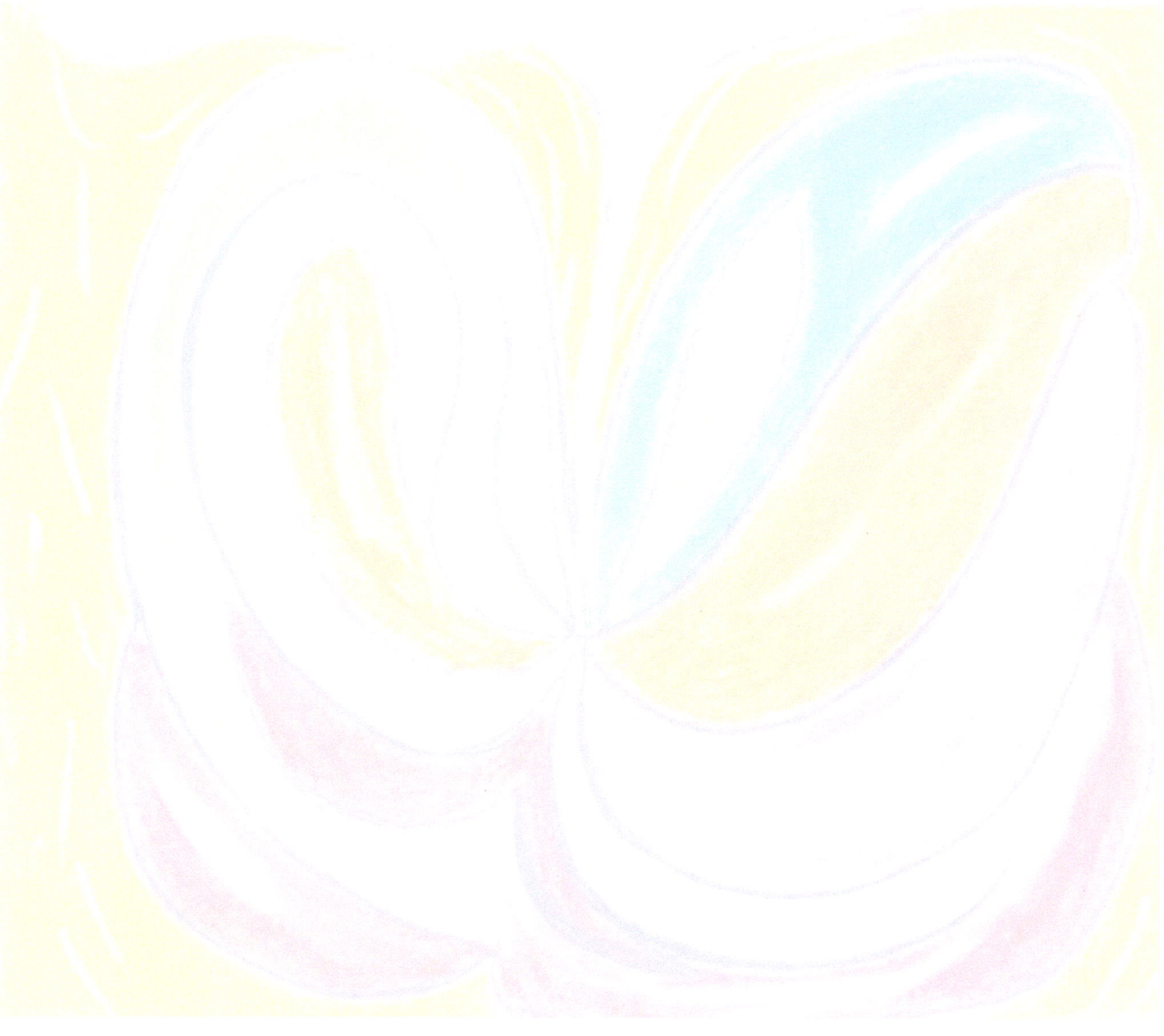

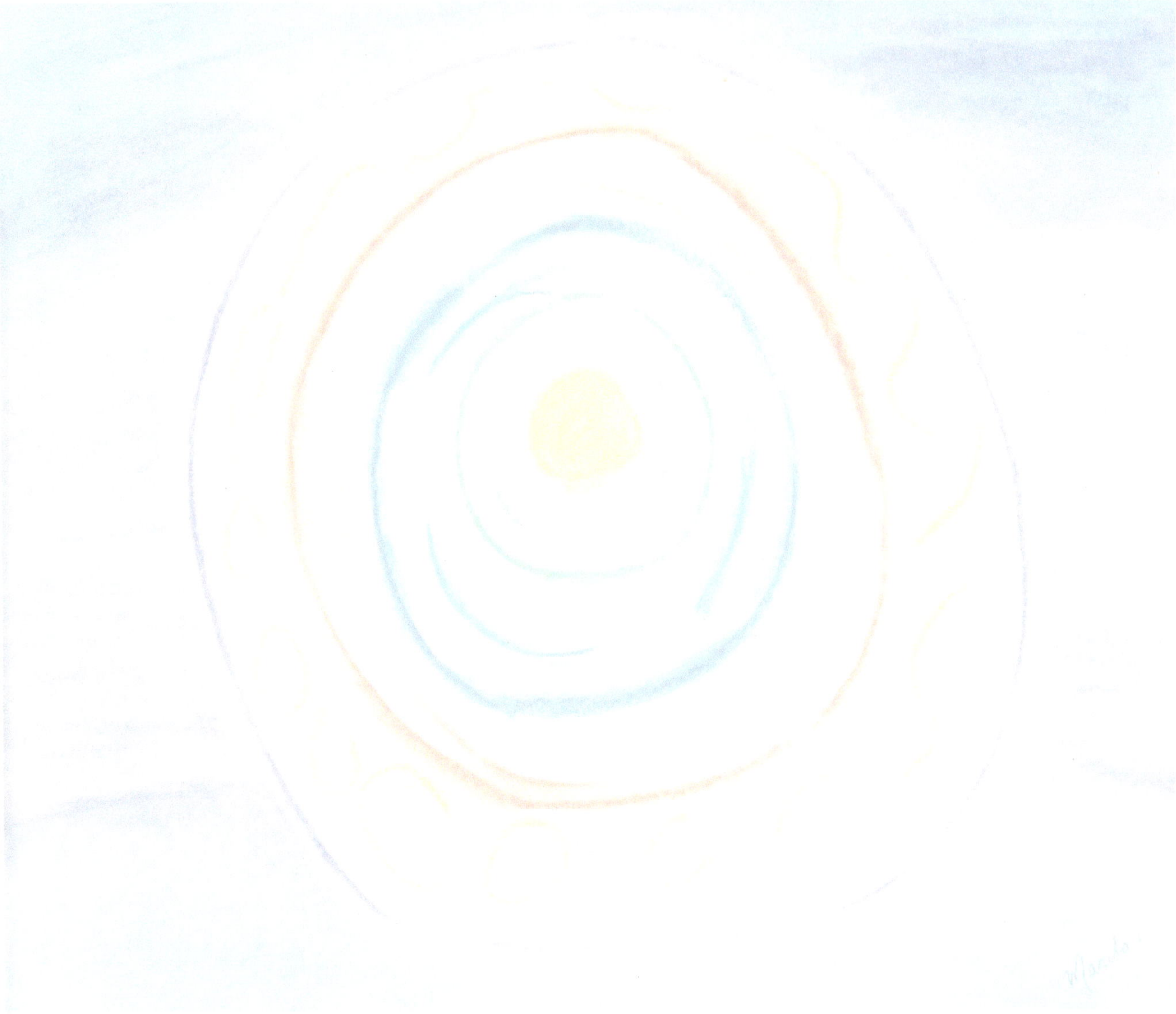

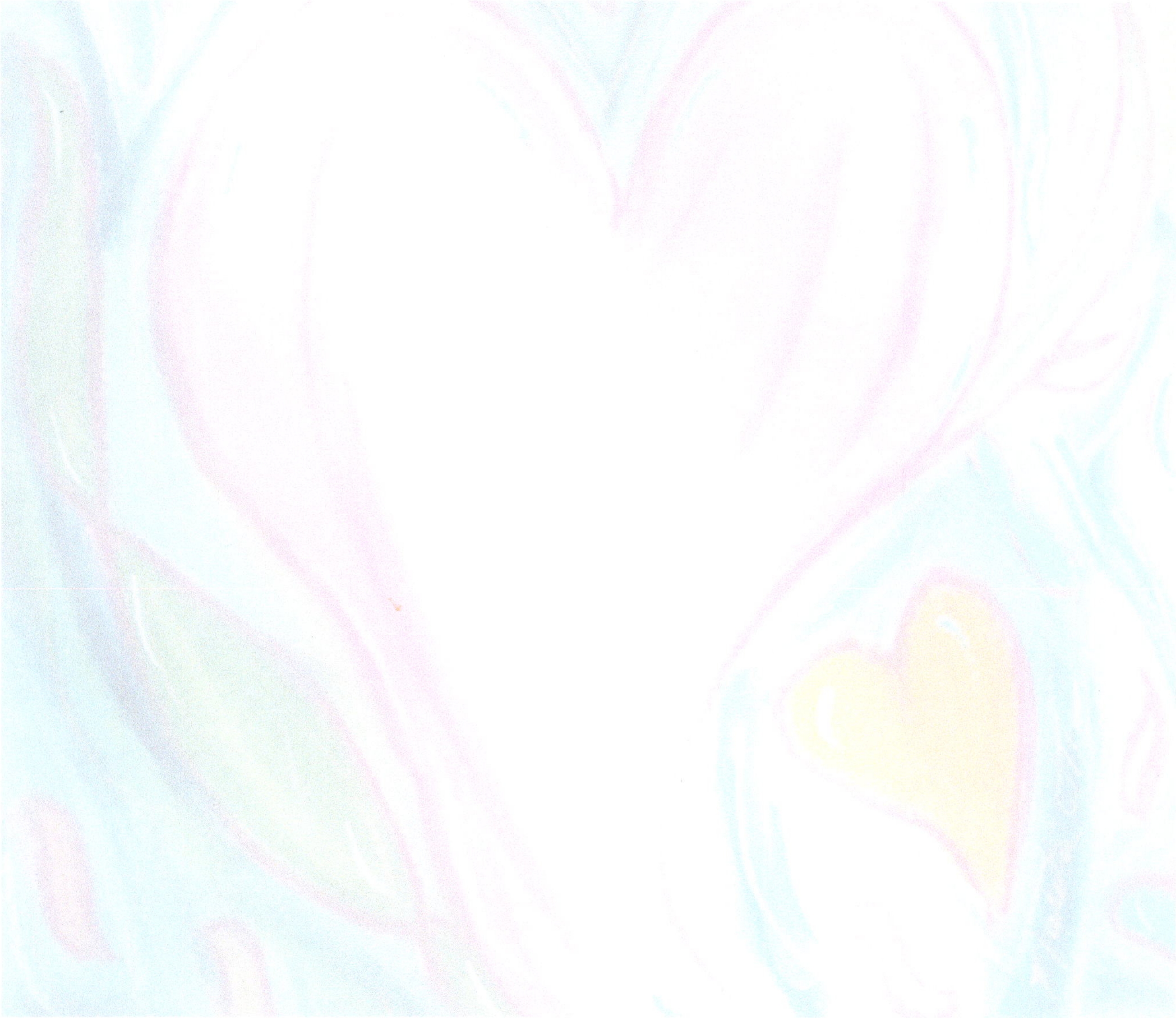

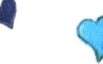 

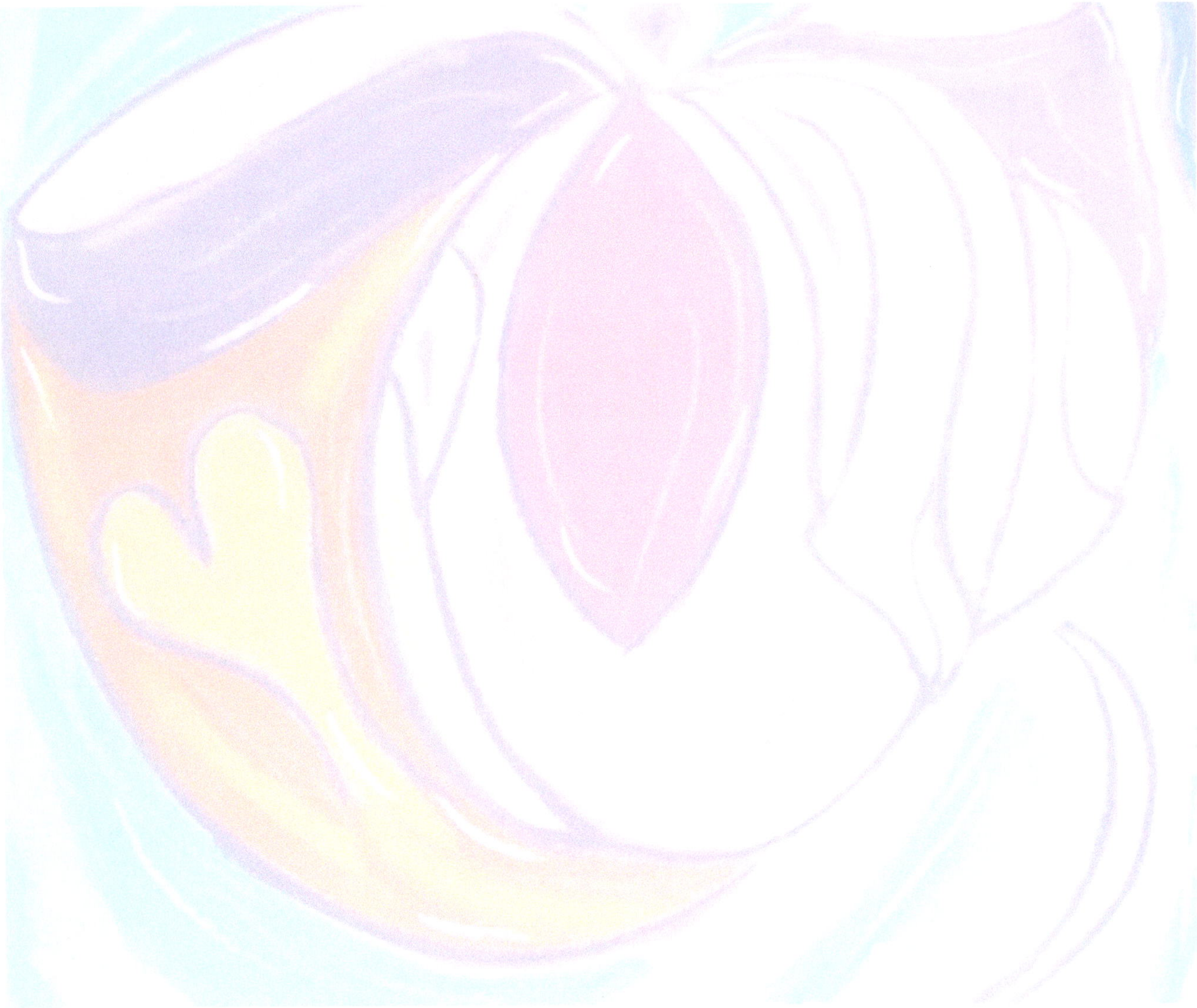

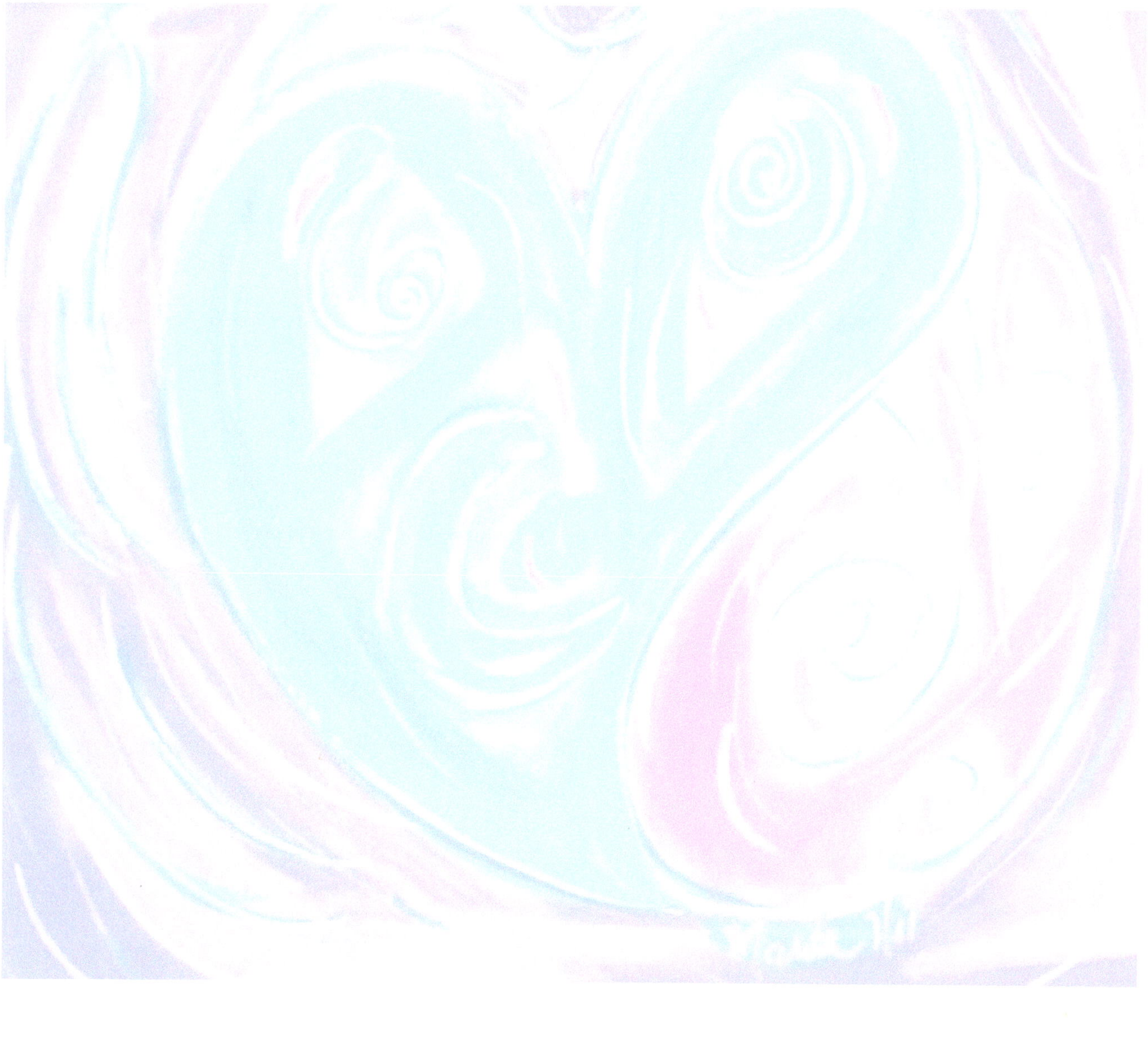

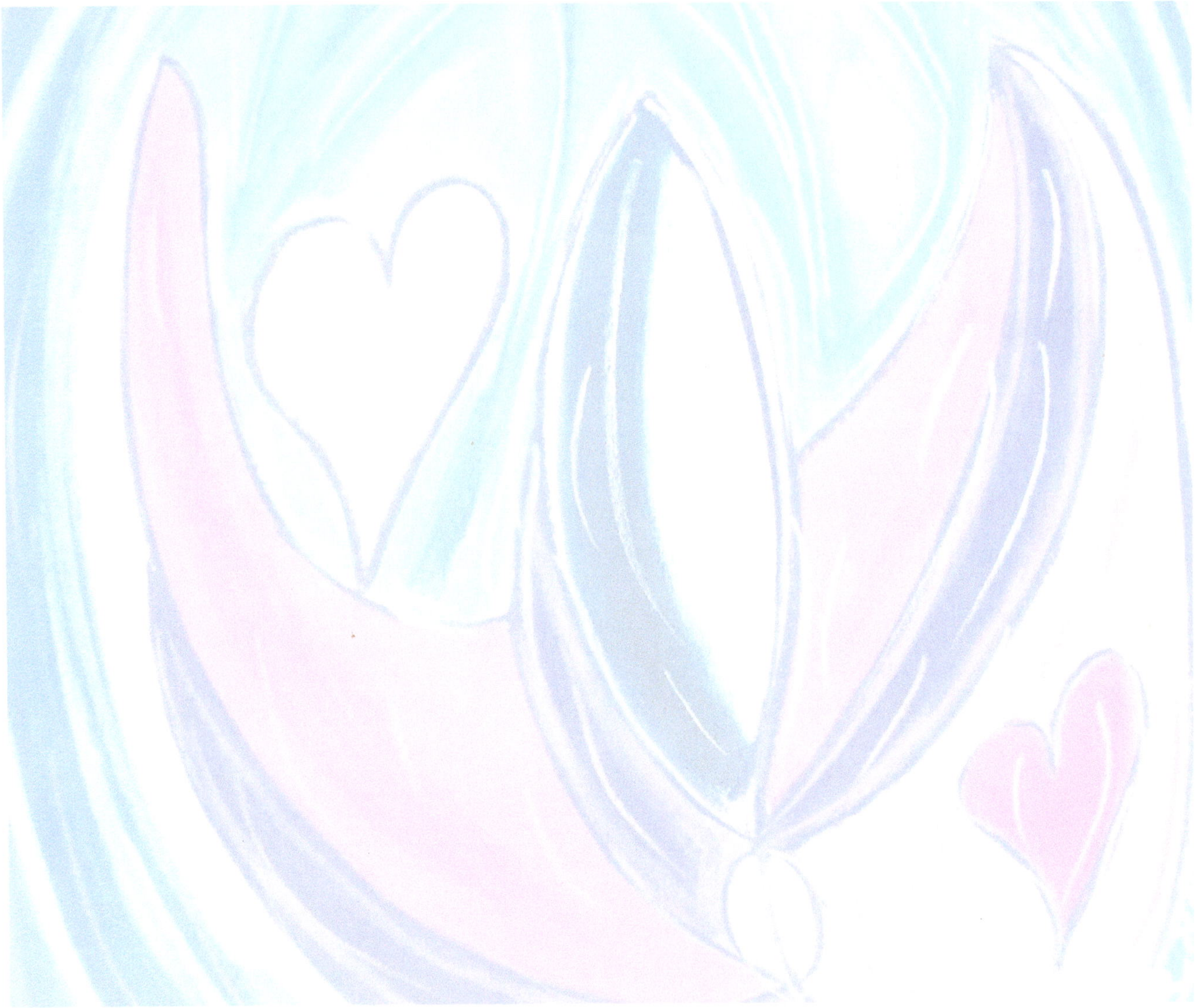

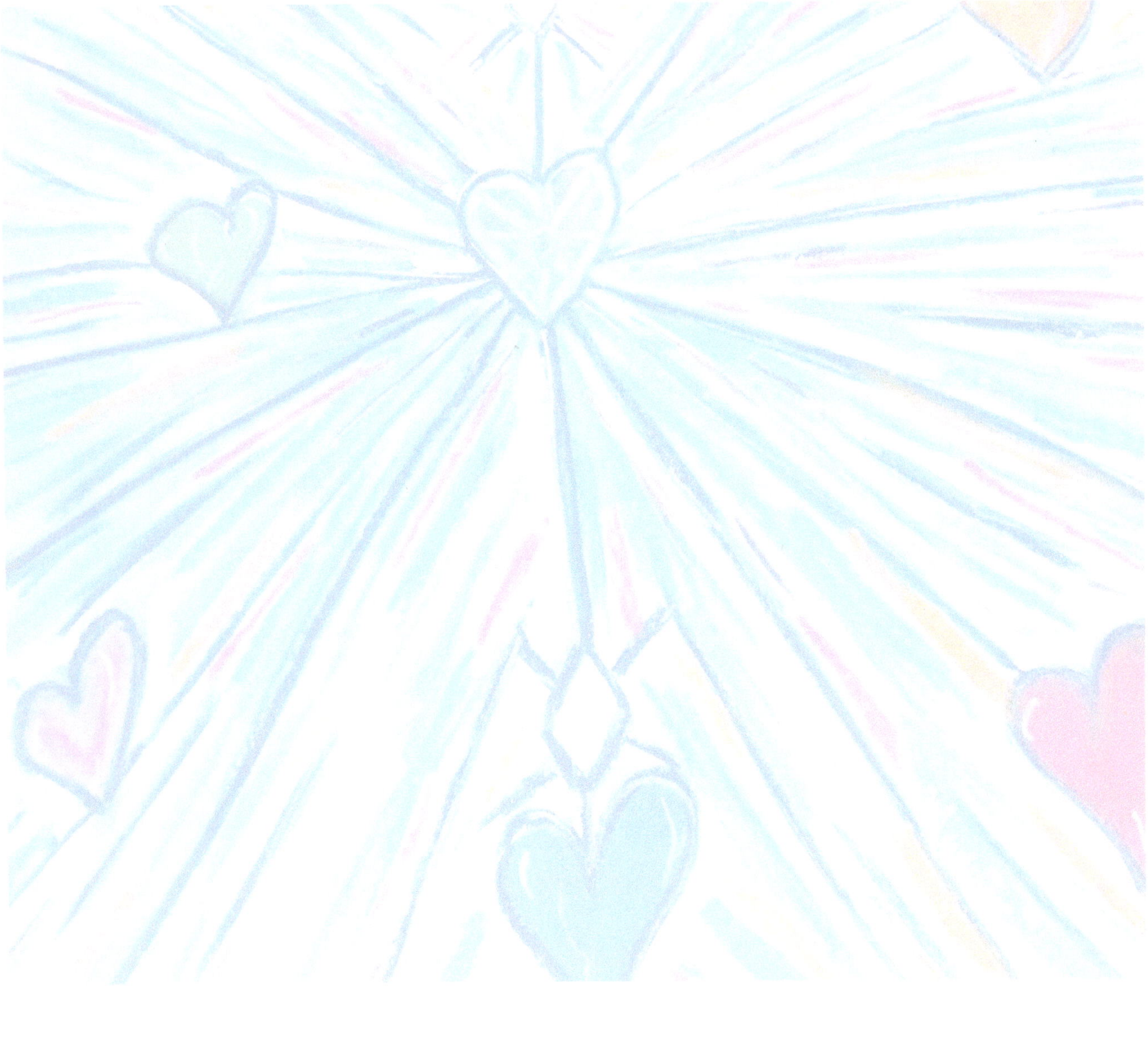

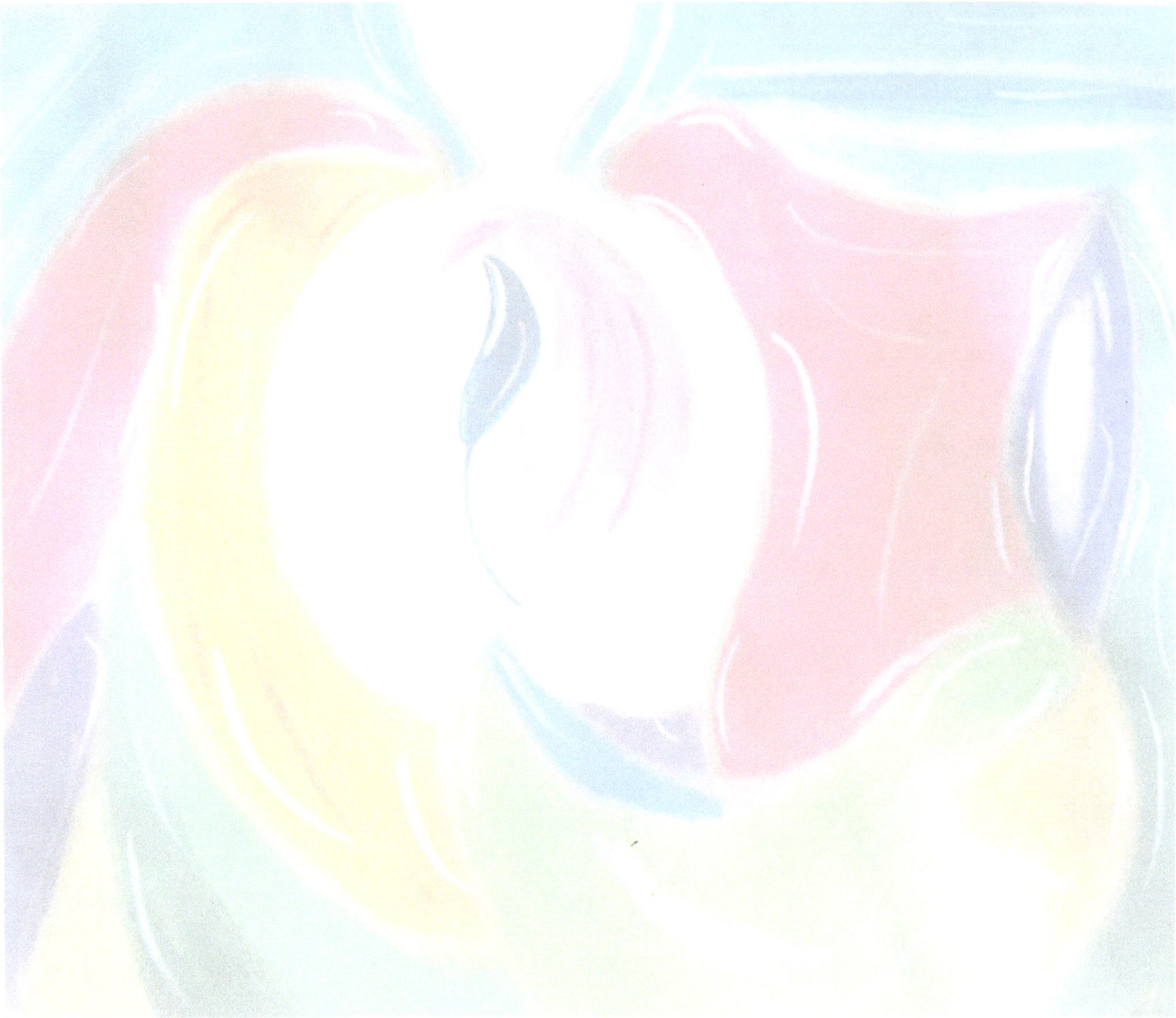

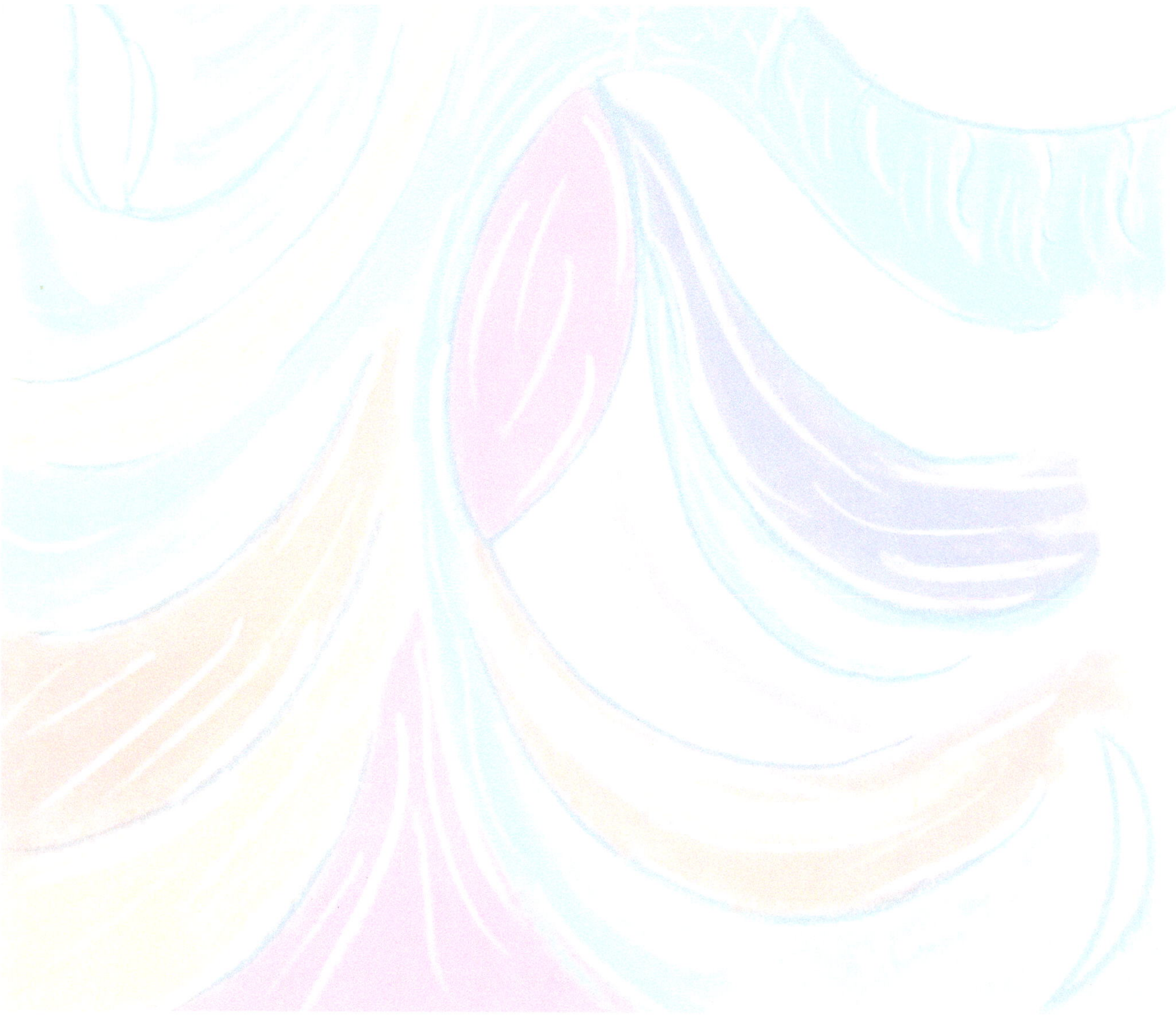

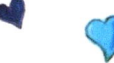

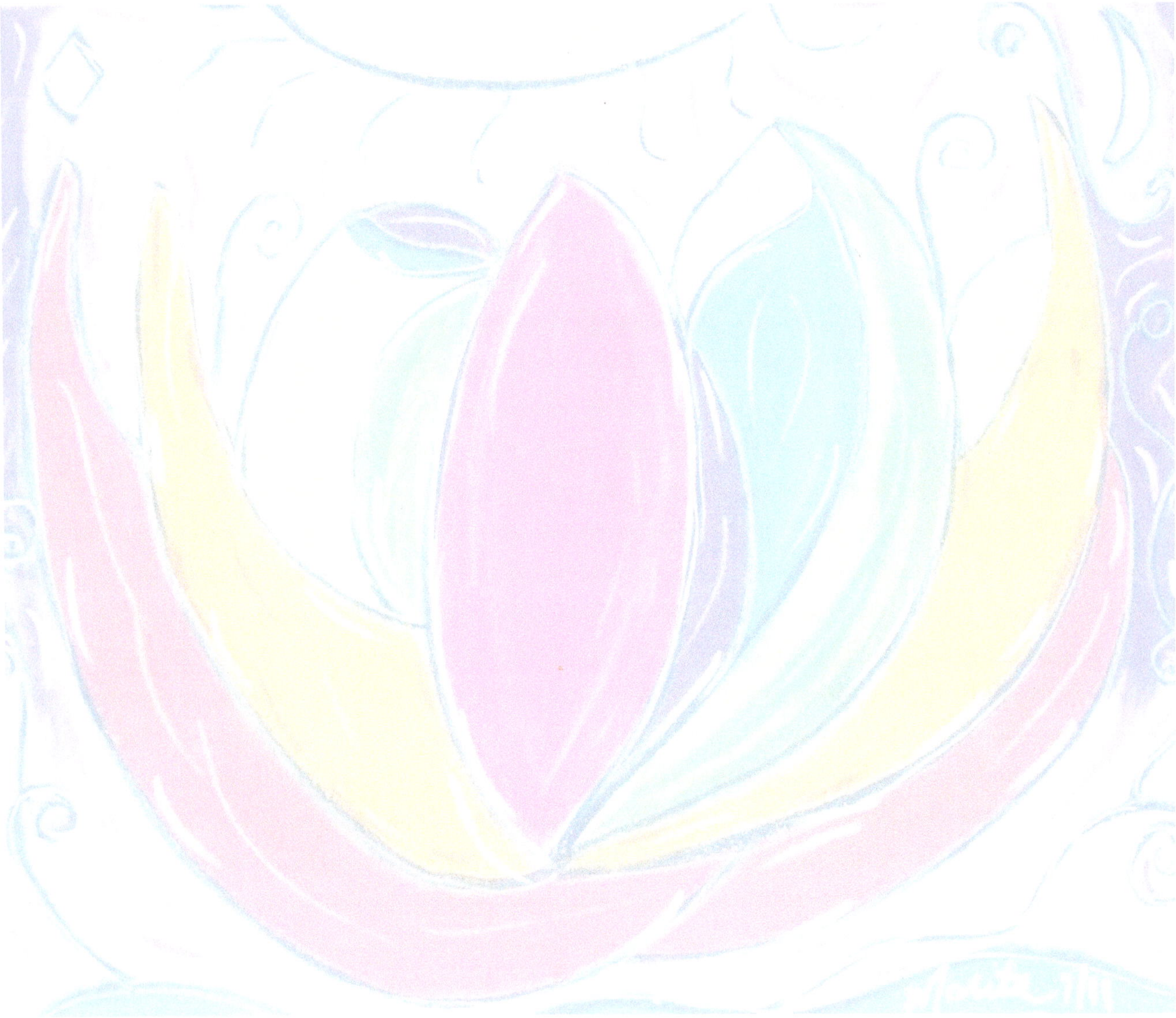

Forgiveness is the way of cleansing the soul

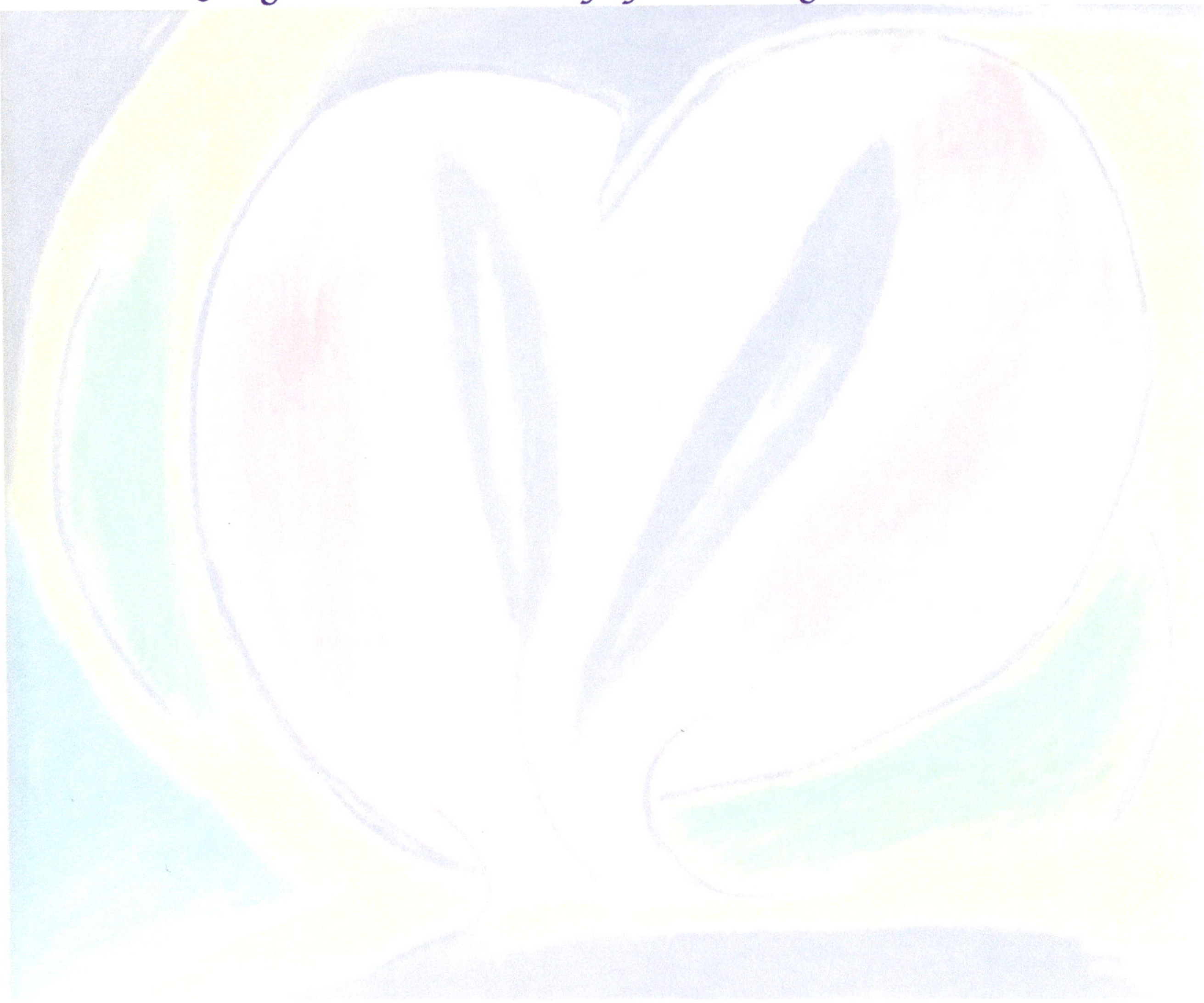

So it moves the way it was meant to move - with pure joy!

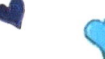 

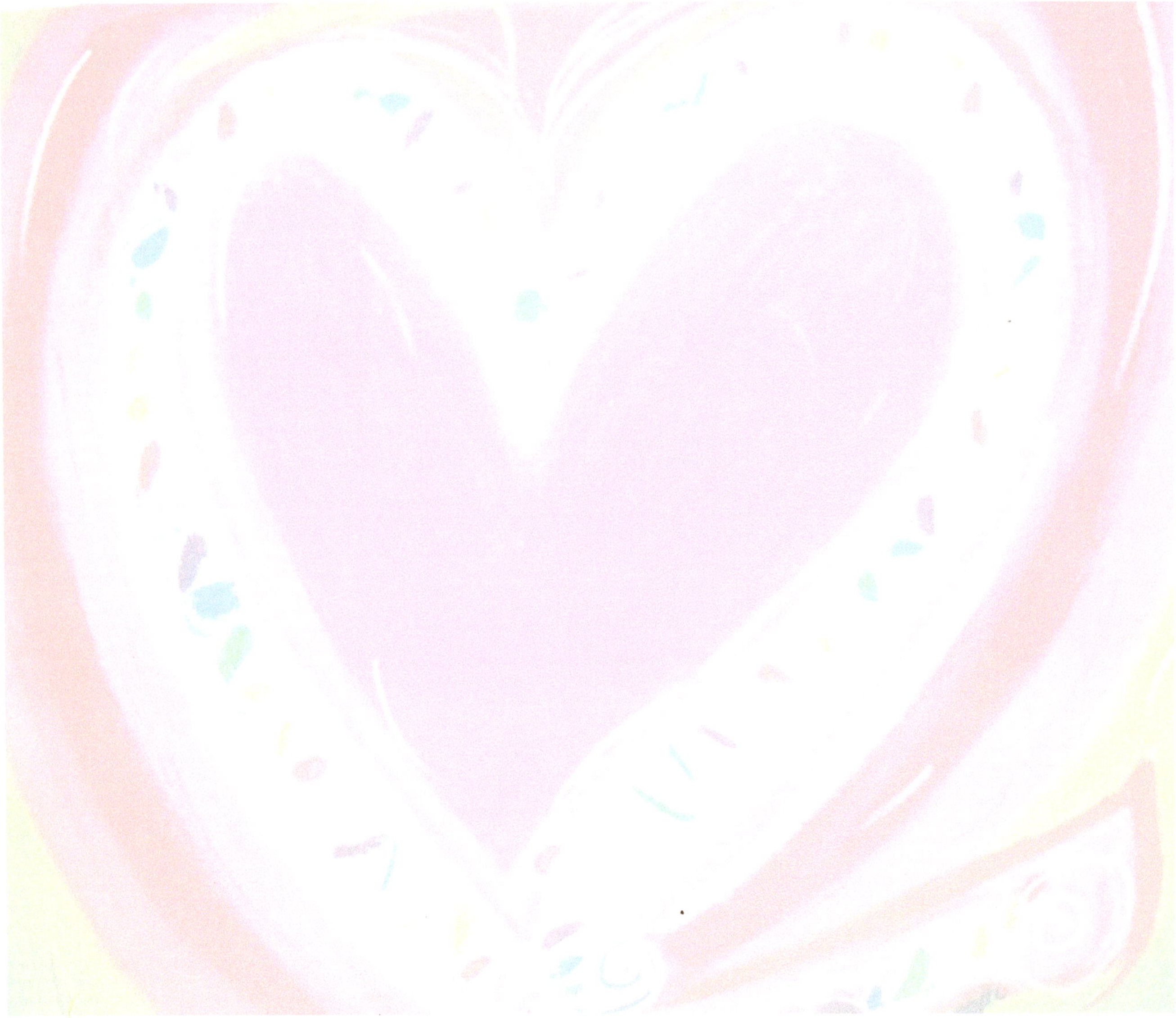

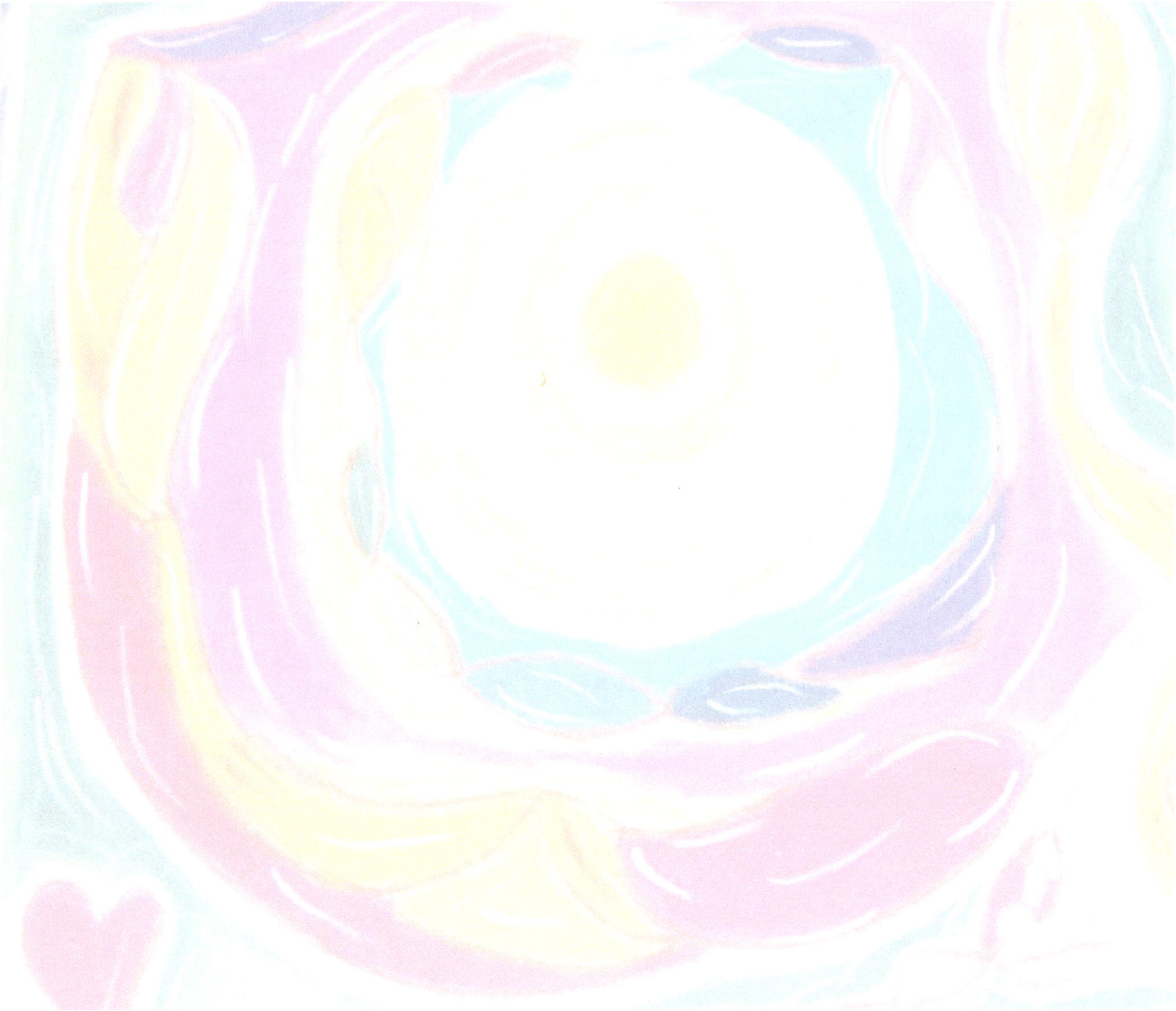

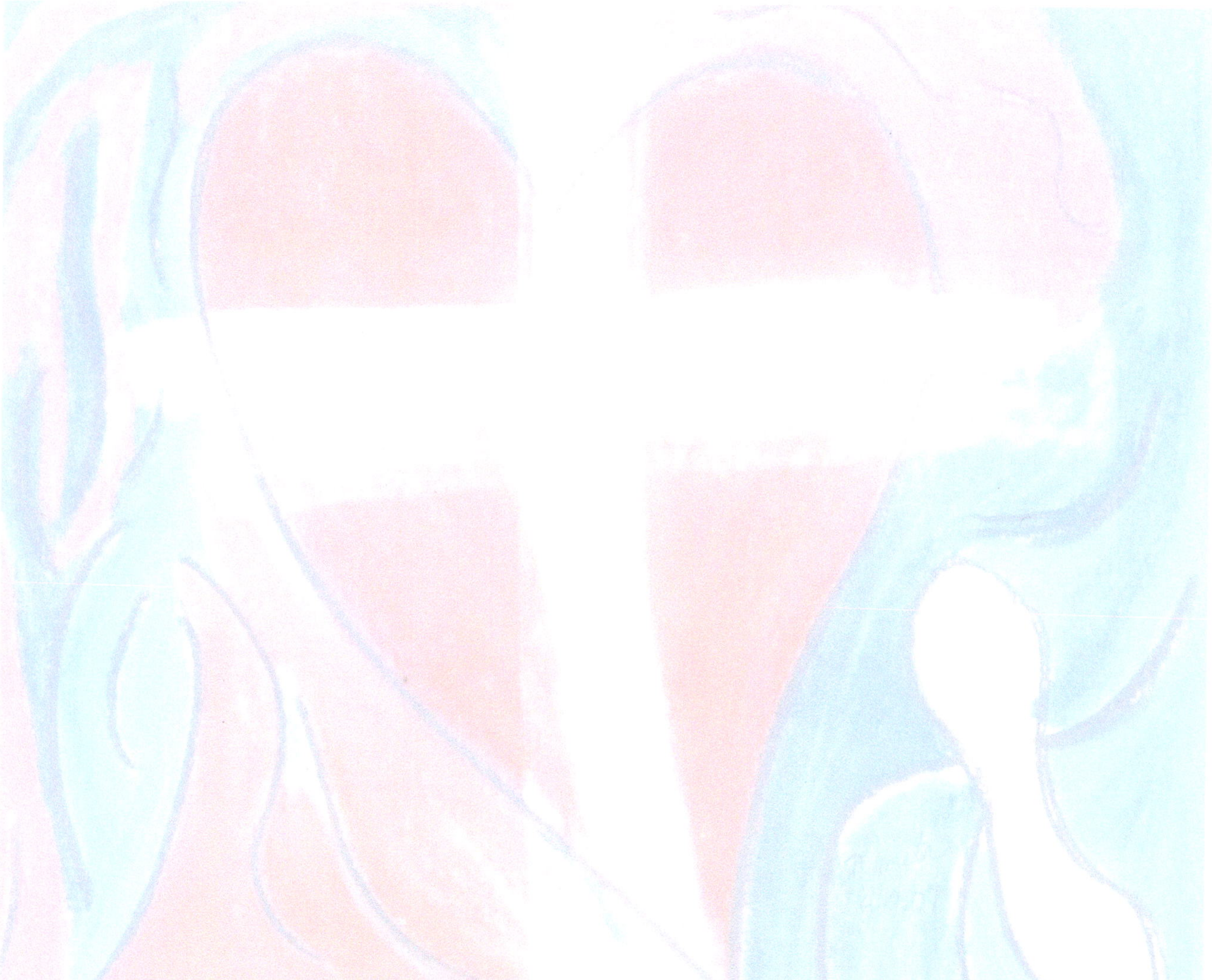

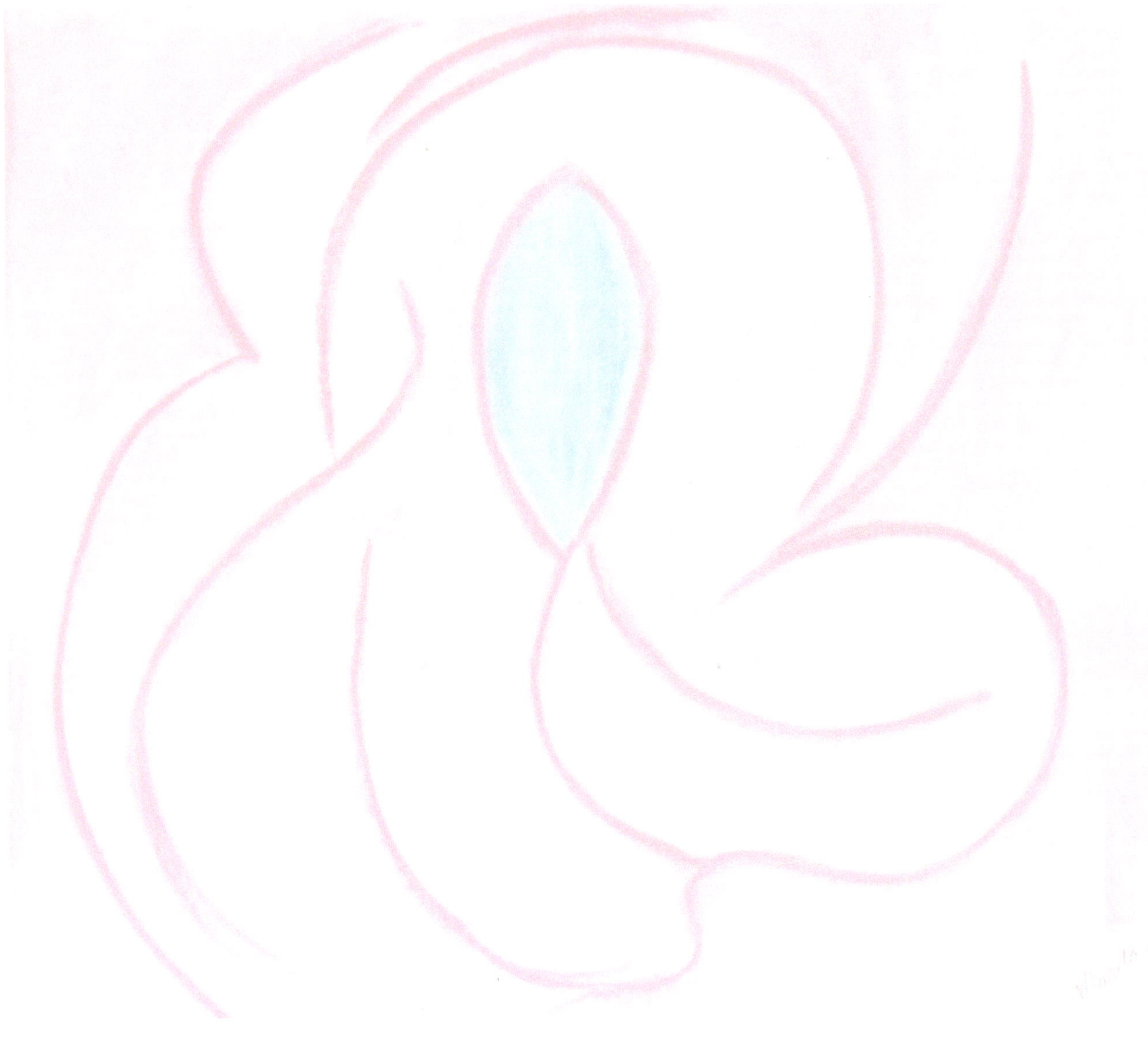

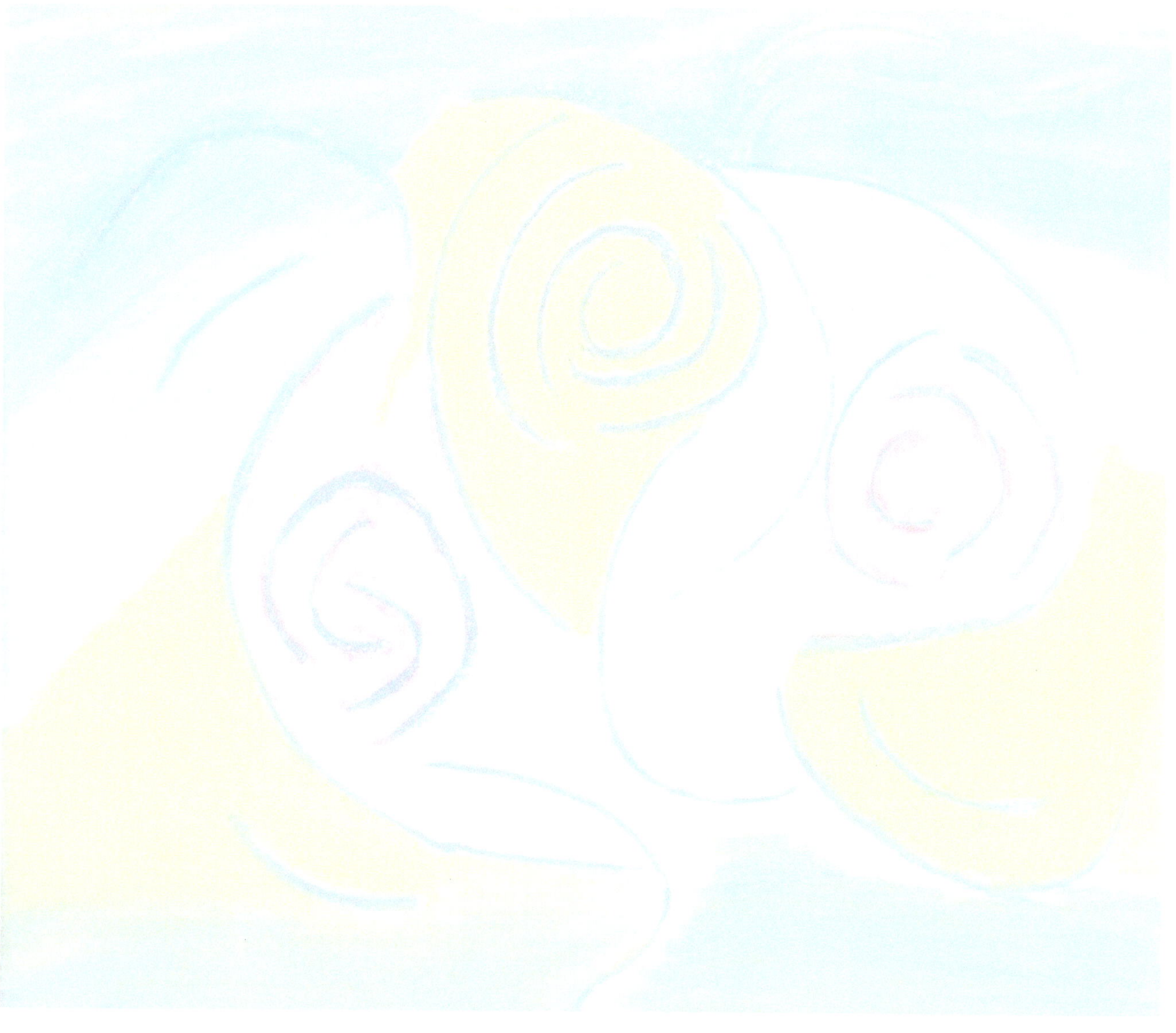

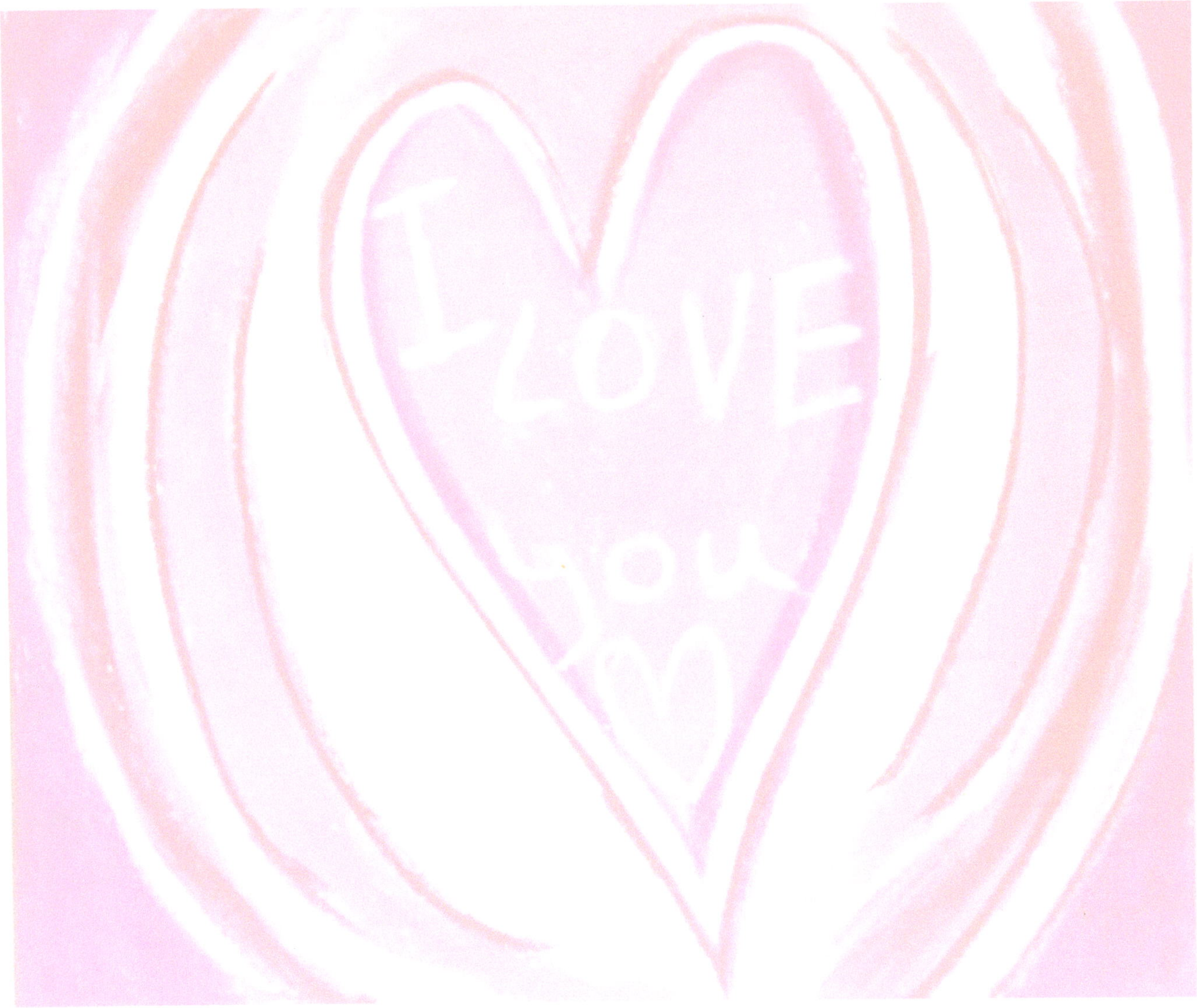

I LOVE
YOU

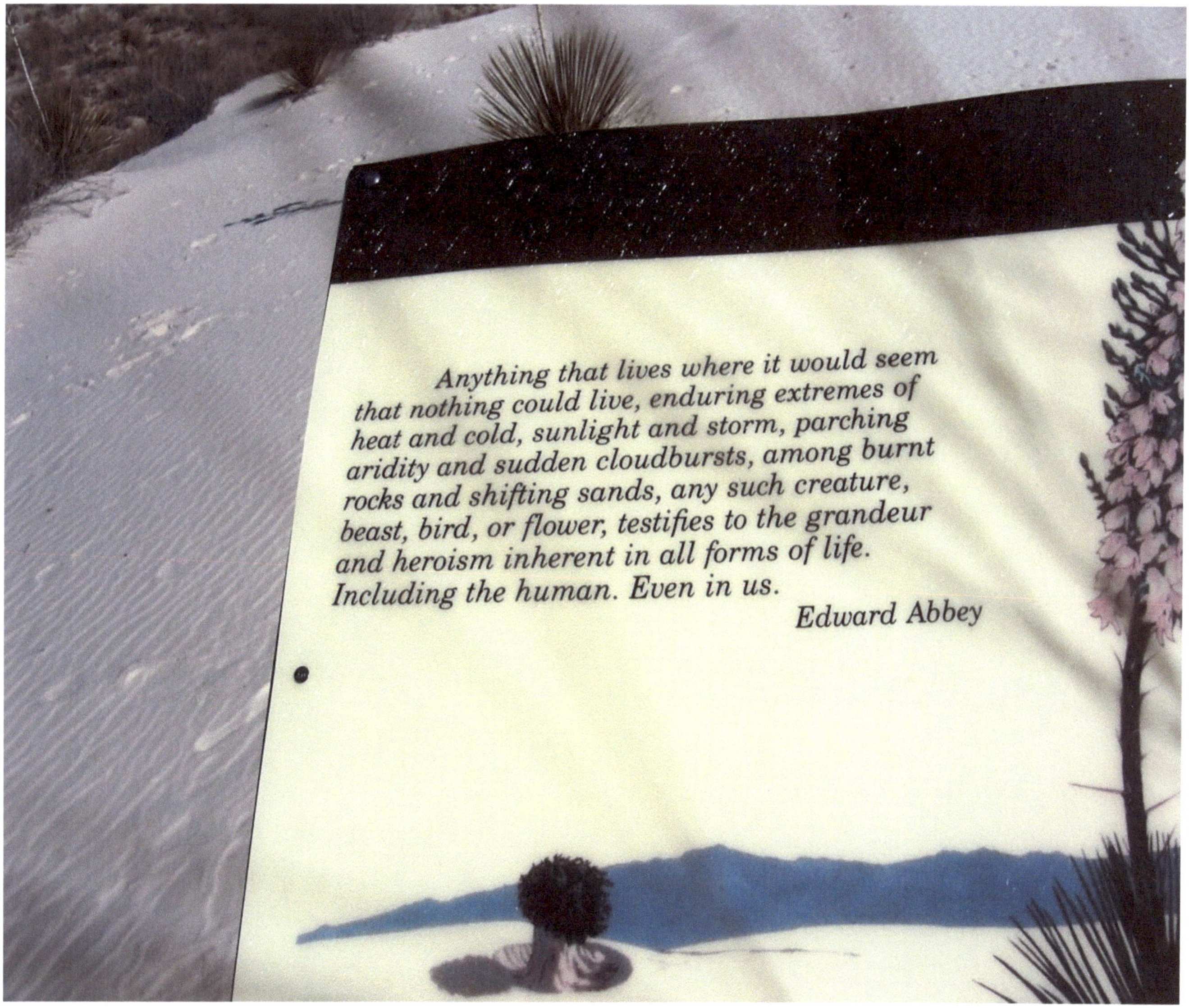

Anything that lives where it would seem
that nothing could live, enduring extremes of
heat and cold, sunlight and storm, parching
aridity and sudden cloudbursts, among burnt
rocks and shifting sands, any such creature,
beast, bird, or flower, testifies to the grandeur
and heroism inherent in all forms of life.
Including the human. Even in us.

Edward Abbey

Embrace this new life and go with it.

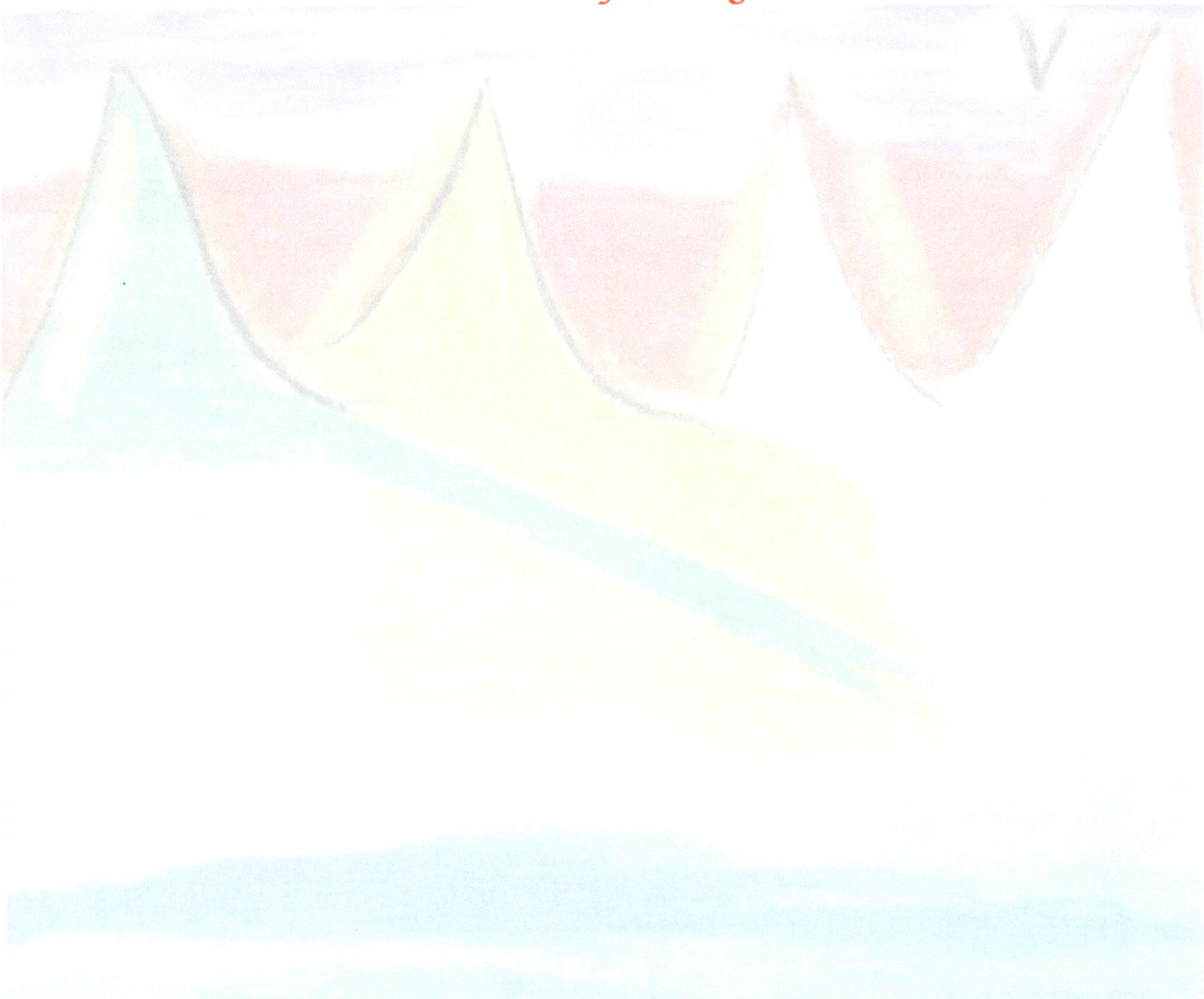

Cry those river of tears that will empty out

into a greater ocean of life.

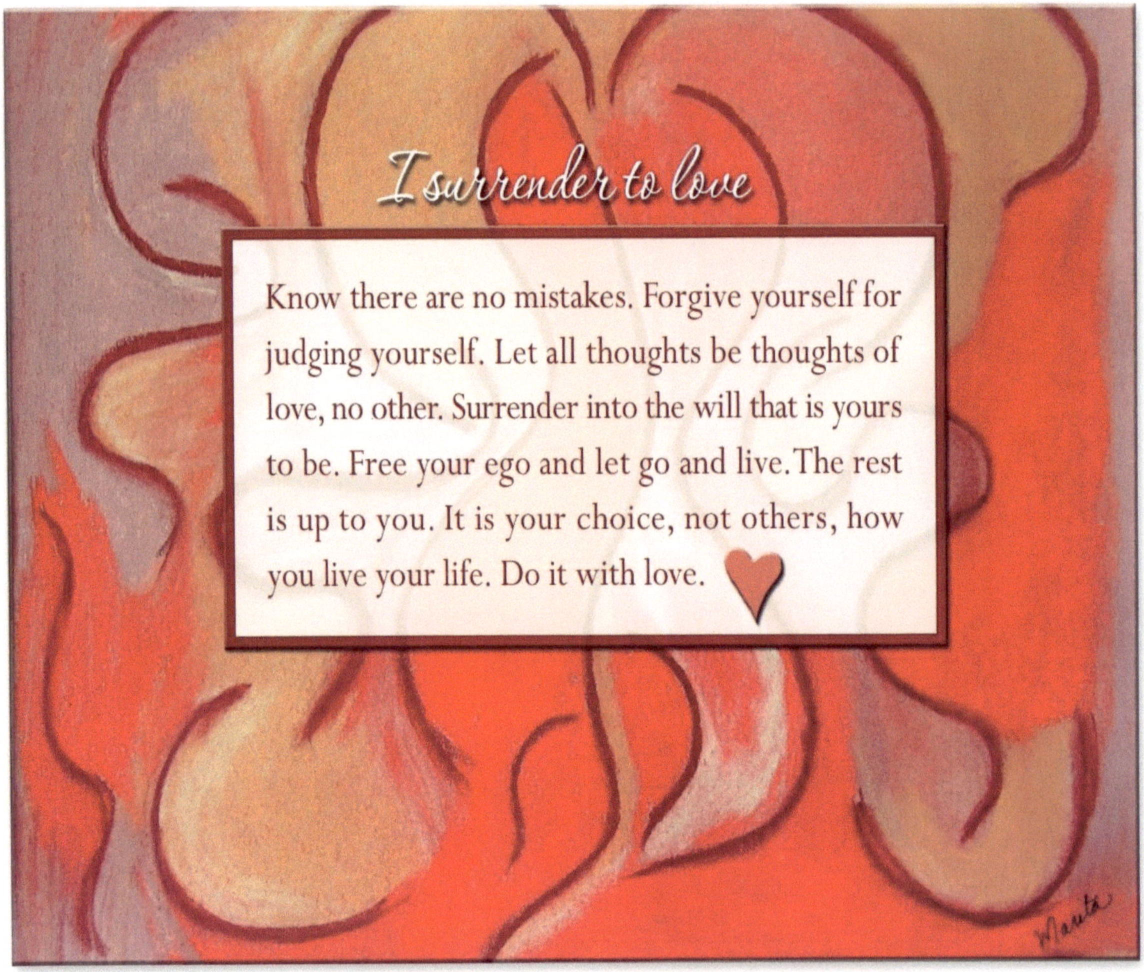

I surrender to love

Know there are no mistakes. Forgive yourself for judging yourself. Let all thoughts be thoughts of love, no other. Surrender into the will that is yours to be. Free your ego and let go and live. The rest is up to you. It is your choice, not others, how you live your life. Do it with love.

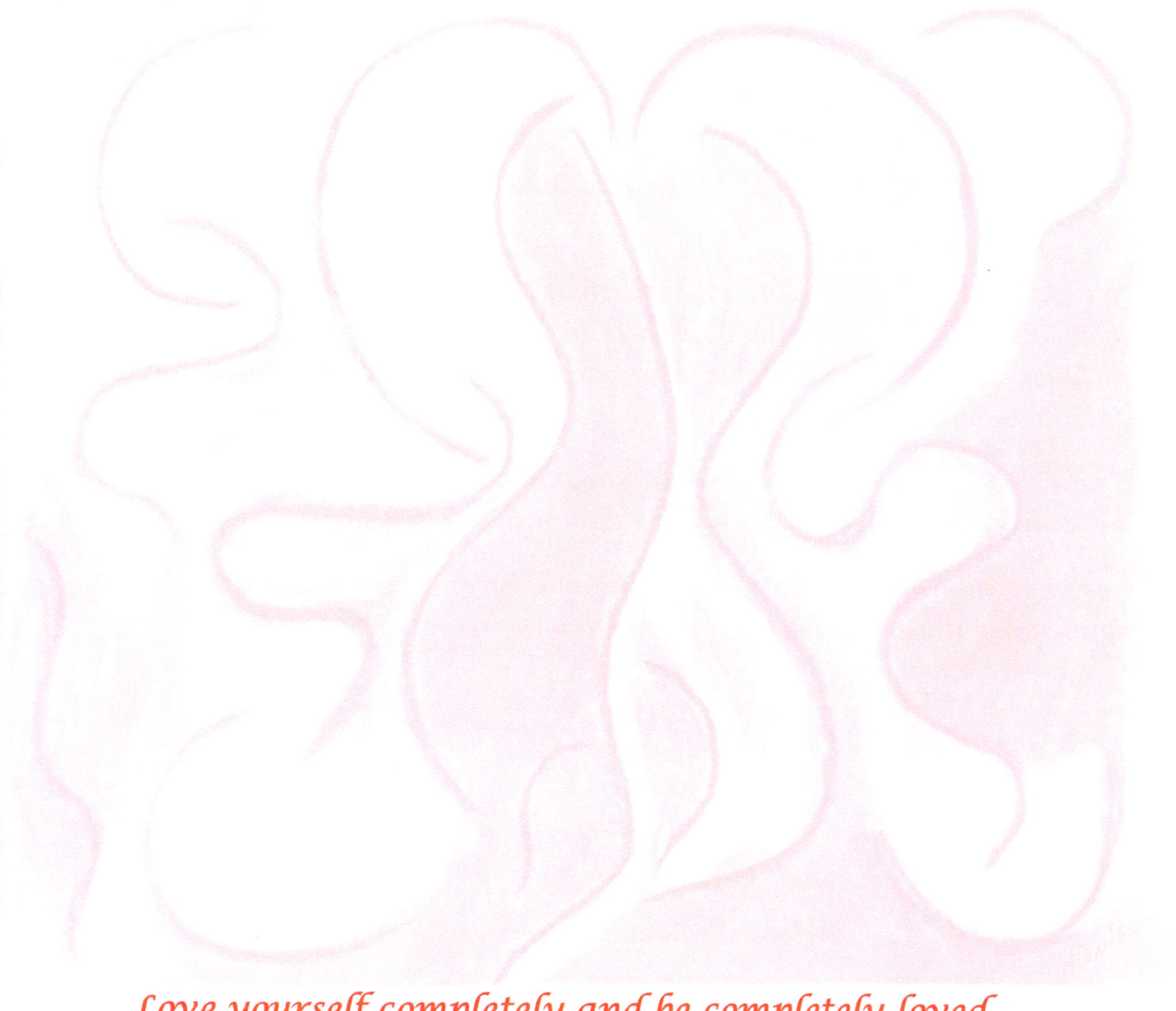

Love yourself completely and be completely loved.

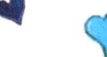 

ABOUT THE AUTHOR

I am currently calling Sedona, Arizona home. I moved to the Sedona area in November 2009 in my Honda Civic with everything I owned to continue to pursue life as an artist/poet and writer trusting in my inner guidance to lead the way.

My passion is connecting with people creating what I call energy art portraits. I connect to a person's higher self and then use chalk pastels to make brilliant colors flow onto the page revealing an expression of the person's feelings Each portrait also includes a poem. I feel a remarkable connection and each experience has been unique and amazing.

I now create journals using the drawings I have done of people, pets and places as watermarks. This journal was created to inspire forgiveness through journaling.

For more information regarding workshops, poems or energy art drawings please contact me at 928-274-4338 or maritagale@gmail.com or my website wisdomandartfromtheheart.com.

.

www.ingramcontent.com/pod-product-compliance
Lightning Source LLC
Chambersburg PA
CBHW050810180526
45159CB00004B/1617